I0458794

THE TRIUMPH OF CHRIST REVELATION UNSEALED

By Tommy McNeill

ISBN (Paperback): 978-1-967951-01-7

ISBN (eBook): 978-1-967951-00-0

ISBN (Hardcover): 978-1-967951-03-1

Published by Sharon Rose Garden Publications

www.spiritualpreterism.com

Scripture quotations are from the King James Version (KJV) of the Bible.

This book is a theological work and is intended solely for educational and inspirational purposes.

Library of Congress Control Number: 2025919149

Printed in the United States of America

First Edition

Contents

PREFACE

From Fear to Fulfillment

The Turning Point

"The Revelation of Jesus Christ, which God gave unto him, to show unto his servants things which must shortly come to pass…" [1] (Revelation 1:1)

For years, I lived beneath a shadow, a dread cast not by tragedy, but by theology. I found myself feverishly poring over prophecy charts, timelines, and headlines—searching, decoding, and finding only heaviness. My faith was guided more by anxious speculation than by the reassuring Spirit. But then, everything shifted. It felt as if a single brick was pulled from a towering wall of tradition. The fortress of fear collapsed, replaced by a breathtaking vision. Revelation became not a cryptic countdown, but a radiant revealing of Him who conquered death, redeemed humanity, and reigns gloriously now. This called me to lift my eyes to the reigning King. This book emerged from that moment of clarity. I invite you to see it too.

Our journey will be guided by Spiritual Preterism, a perspective that understands Revelation's prophecies as already fulfilled in Christ and His Church, emphasizing His present spiritual accomplishments and victories rather than future earthly disasters.

The Triumph of Christ: Revelation Unsealed is my invitation to exchange fear for truth, confusion for clarity, and speculation for spiritual reality. This is a return to Revelation's purpose—every symbol reflecting Jesus, every vision declaring His victory, every page affirming His finished work. We'll explore Christ's spiritual triumph—unlocking symbols long misunderstood. As earlier emphasized, Revelation is a spiritual unveiling of Christ's completed redemptive work. This message of victory stands in stark contrast to fear-based interpretations. It's time to hear it anew.

A Word from the Author's Heart

I believe Revelation has been profoundly misunderstood—overshadowed by fear, diluted by speculation, distorted by sensationalism. We've viewed its symbols through the wrong lens, turning victory into doom. It's time for clarity—a return to what Revelation truly reveals: Christ's triumph.

Rather than rigid theory, this lens—Spiritual Preterism—invites deeper spiritual insight. Christ is not waiting to reign; He is revealed as victorious now.

These truths came through years of seeking, praying, and pressing forward. I can assure you that it didn't come from my worthiness. I don't claim perfection. I'm still learning, growing, listening. My aim is simply to magnify Jesus, elevate the truth of His completed work, and help others exchange fear for victory.

I didn't write this as a scholar. I wrote it as someone set free—and I invite you to see what I saw.

May these pages ignite your spirit, challenge every assumption, and draw you irresistibly closer to Jesus.

Together, let's grow deeper into His grace and clearer into His victory—for His truth is marching on.

What you're about to discover will shift how you see not just Revelation, but the entire redemptive arc of Scripture.

—Tommy McNeill

---

[1] All Scripture quotations in this book are taken from the King James Version (KJV) of the Bible.

INTRODUCTION

A Spiritual Lens on Revelation

What if everything you've been taught about Revelation is not just incomplete, but entirely upside down?

For generations, the final book of the Bible was approached with trembling hands, taught as foretelling unstoppable disasters, monstrous rulers, and unleashed divine wrath.

I lived in that mindset—consistently tracking prophecy timelines, matching headlines to cryptic symbols, and bracing for catastrophe.

But then, Revelation turned inside out. Everything changed as I revisited the Scriptures through the lens of Christ's finished work. Fear turned to awe. Dread turned to worship. Anxiety became adoration.

What if Revelation was never a puzzle of destruction, but a portrait of the Christ, the Messiah?

For many, this perspective may be new or even challenging, especially if you've been accustomed to a futurist view. That is understandable. Our aim is simply to present a Christ-centered understanding rooted deeply in Scripture, inviting an open heart and mind as we explore what Revelation truly unveils.

In a world increasingly consumed by anxieties about the future, headlines often seem to echo age-old fears of calamity and chaos. This interpretation of Revelation offers a profound counter-narrative, inviting us to exchange dread for worship and speculation for spiritual reality. It is a timely message of peace, present victory, and a deeply rooted hope that transcends fleeting earthly concerns, revealing a King who reigns gloriously now.

"But this man, after he had offered one sacrifice for sins forever, sat down on the right hand of God...

For by one offering he hath perfected forever them that are sanctified." (Hebrews 10:12–14)

His work is complete.

His reign is now.

The Revelation of Jesus Christ is unsealed.

What Makes This Book Different

Unlike many commentaries that view Revelation as a future roadmap of disasters, this book offers a fundamentally different lens: a Christ-centered unveiling of prophecies already fulfilled in the life of Jesus and a celebration of His present, triumphant Kingdom.

Eschatology Perspectives

While many books offer comprehensive surveys of eschatological systems—futurism, historicism, idealism, and various forms of preterism—this is not one of them. If you're seeking a deep comparative analysis, there is no shortage of scholarly material available. Instead, this book offers a singular focus: unveiling the spiritual triumph of Christ through the lens of Scripture. Our aim is not to weigh every theory, but to lift the veil—so that Jesus may be seen in all His glory.

"Neither shall they say, Lo Here! Or, Lo There! for, behold, the kingdom of God is within you." (Luke 17:21)

"We receiving a kingdom which cannot be moved." (Hebrews 12:28)

We aren't awaiting a kingdom's arrival; we're living in the victory of Christ and His kingdom.

Like Nicodemus, many approach God's mysteries literally. When Jesus said, "Except a man be born again…" (John 3:3), Nicodemus asked, "can he enter the second time into his mother's womb, and be born?" He missed the spiritual truth.

Similarly, Revelation can be misunderstood when we fixate too literally on beasts and calamities. Jesus explained the kingdom "cometh not with observation." (Luke 17:20)

Only spiritual eyes can grasp that Revelation is not predicting physical ruin—it reveals spiritual triumph.

Until our vision shifts—as Nicodemus' did—we may miss what Jesus unveils, both then and now.

This book guides you through Revelation's fulfilled realities—from Old Testament apostate Jerusalem's fall to the New Jerusalem's bridal descension.

You'll see the beast not as a future tyrant, but as a works-based system Christ conquered. See bowls and trumpets as spiritual judgments on the system rejecting its Savior.

These are proclamations, not predictions.

"Who hath delivered us… into the kingdom of his dear Son." (Colossians 1:13)

Spiritual Preterism: Beyond Historical Fulfillment

Classical Preterism primarily focuses on historical fulfillments, usually anchored in tangible historical events. While it emphasizes past fulfillment, it often does so largely in political or literal historical terms. In contrast, Spiritual Preterism shifts the focus from mere historical milestones to enduring spiritual realities, such as the current reign of Christ in believers' hearts, the living nature of the New Jerusalem as the spiritually alive Church today, and the internal, transformative victory over sin and spiritual death already accomplished by Jesus.

Therefore, Spiritual Preterism does not merely look backward to historical fulfillment; it calls believers forward into a vibrant, victorious experience of Christ's Kingdom. This approach invites believers not only to understand Revelation, but to live daily in the power of its spiritually fulfilled truths.

This book's focus is that the symbolic judgments within Revelation were spiritually fulfilled by Jesus, primarily through the cross, thereby ending the Old Covenant age.

Additionally, it is important to emphasize that Spiritual Preterism derives its interpretation of Revelation exclusively from the Scriptures themselves. While the Olivet Discourse and portions of Revelation chapters 6 and 7 clearly align with the historical judgment on Jerusalem in AD 70, other detailed physical events surrounding that historical occurrence are primarily documented outside of Scripture (e.g., the historical writings of Josephus).

However, this interpretive framework consciously refrains from relying upon such external historical sources for the interpretation of Revelation. Instead, Spiritual Preterism remains firmly anchored in scriptural revelation alone, interpreting the seals and other symbolic elements spiritually, emphasizing their significance within Christ's accomplished work and ongoing spiritual kingdom.

Thus, readers should understand clearly: while historical references can offer context, they are never the foundation or authority for interpreting Revelation within Spiritual Preterism. Our foundation and interpretive lens remain solely and entirely the inspired Word of God.

How to Read This Book

The Triumph of Christ: Revelation Unsealed is not a typical commentary on Revelation. It is a lens-shifting journey—one that invites you to see the final book of the Bible not as a forecast of doom, but as a spiritual illumination of Christ by His Revelation.

To help you navigate this unique perspective, here are a few guiding principles:

1. Read Through a Spiritual Lens

Previously explained, this approach interprets Revelation as unveiling what Christ has already accomplished spiritually.

Ask yourself as you read:

"What does this reveal about Jesus, His Kingdom, and the covenantal fulfillment from the Old to the New?"

2. Let Scripture Interpret Scripture

Rather than relying on charts or speculation, this work roots every interpretation in the Bible itself—especially the Old Testament prophecies, the Gospels, and the writings of Paul and the prophets.

You'll see frequent cross-references. Don't rush past them.

Follow them when possible—they are the keys to unlocking the imagery of Revelation.

3. Take Time to Reflect

The chapters are theologically rich and spiritually layered. Don't be afraid to pause, reflect, reread, and pray. Revelation was never meant to be read like a thriller—but like a heavenly scroll opening truth by truth, line by line.

4. Read with an Open Heart, Not Just an Analytical Mind

This book is not just about understanding Revelation. It's about seeing Jesus unveiled—not as a future warrior, but as a present, reigning King. This perspective may challenge long-held assumptions, especially if you have been steeped in a futurist view. Therefore, I invite you to approach these pages not with defensiveness, but with an open heart, asking the Spirit for guidance.

5. See Yourself in the Story

Revelation is not about escape. It's about inheritance.

You are not a spectator in the last days. You are a citizen of the Kingdom, a participant in Christ's triumph, and a living stone in the New Jerusalem.

This book will call you not just to understand, but to walk in the light of the Lamb today.

A Final Encouragement

If something feels unfamiliar, don't reject it too quickly. Let the Spirit illuminate the text. As you turn these pages, you may just discover that Revelation is not the Church's nightmare. It is her song of fulfilled promise—her anthem of inheritance.

Chapter 1

SHIFTING PERSPECTIVES: TRADING FEAR FOR VICTORY

The Divine Puzzle: From Fragments to Fulfillment

Have you ever tried to assemble a puzzle without the picture on the box?

You arrange each piece, hoping something recognizable will emerge—but the picture remains hidden. For years I stared at Revelation's scattered pieces with mounting spiritual unease. I was missing the central masterpiece—Christ's already-accomplished victory.

God's people and the Old Testament prophets shared this very struggle.

They held prophetic fragments and mysterious promises, each hinting at something magnificent, yet the picture stayed incomplete.

Then came Revelation—God's divine masterpiece.

With it, the final pieces clicked into place, and at the center, radiant and unmistakable, stood Jesus Christ.

Like many, I once approached Revelation with fear, reading it as a roadmap to disaster. But when I began to see it through the lens of Christ and His finished work, the chaos gave way to clarity. The Spirit illuminated what tradition had obscured, and what once felt ominous now overflows with hope.

For me, the shift began with the revelation of the New Jerusalem.

I no longer saw it as a distant city in the sky but as the Bride of Christ—the living, breathing Church, and Kingdom of God.

That was the missing piece. And once it clicked, everything else fell into place.

The Heartbeat of Revelation: A Present Victory

Revelation unveils Jesus as the triumphant King, reigning now and forever.

This is the Bible's conclusion—it is its crown.

Prophecy, promise, and vision converge in one glorious theme: the manifestation of Jesus Christ.

He is the Alpha and Omega.

The Prophetic Masterpiece: Threads of Redemption

Throughout the ages, prophets glimpsed fragments of this masterpiece.

Isaiah glimpsed the New Jerusalem as a radiant city whose walls were Salvation; Daniel saw a mysterious stone cut without hands that would grow into an eternal Kingdom; and Ezekiel described a life-giving river flowing from the temple of God.

How would it all unfold? What was God's endgame?

Revelation brings the answer.

It gathers scattered visions into one glorious revelation of Christ—victorious, sovereign, and enthroned.

What was once hazy now radiates with clarity, fixing our eyes on Jesus, the center of redemption's story.

And this unveiling is not merely retrospective—it's a call to live now in His present victory.

Revelation invites you to step back—to see the whole picture through the lens of Christ's triumph.

Like Nicodemus, we must awaken to spiritual sight—to perceive the Kingdom not as future spectacle but as present reality.

Your life, too, is part of God's grand design.

As Paul wrote, "We speak the wisdom of God in a mystery, even the hidden wisdom, which God ordained before the world unto our glory." (1 Corinthians 2:7)

That mystery has now been made manifest in Christ.

The puzzle is complete.

The masterpiece unveiled.

As we continue, you'll see how even the judgments, trumpets, and bowls aren't future calamities, but spiritual signs tied to covenantal transitions. You'll discover how the sealed scroll is not a mystery of doom, but a declaration of Christ's worthiness to redeem, the Revelation of Jesus Christ itself.

The Radiant Centerpiece: The Unveiling of Christ

The word "apocalypse" often conjures images of disaster—earthquakes, fire, plagues, and chaos.

But the word itself means something far more profound.

From the Greek apokalypsis, it simply means unveiling.

And what, exactly, does Revelation unveil?

Not terror, devastation, or a ticking clock toward ruin.

Revelation unveils a triumph. It does not magnify the schemes of darkness—it reveals the triumph of the Lamb.

As Habakkuk prophesied:

"For the earth shall be filled with the knowledge of the glory of the Lord, as the waters cover the sea." (Habakkuk 2:14)

That is the heartbeat of Revelation, the revealing of God's promise fulfilled in Jesus.

In John's visions, Jesus is not merely the suffering servant, He is the enthroned King.

The imagery is rich, layered, and profoundly symbolic, each title showing us a facet of His divine mission.

He is revealed as:

The Lamb who was slain (Revelation 5:6)—the sacrifice that secured eternal redemption.

The Lion of Judah (Revelation 5:5)—roaring with unshakable authority.

The Alpha and the Omega (Revelation 1:8)—the eternal source and culmination of all creation.

These are not poetic decorations.

They are theological foundations—anchors for our faith, revealing who Christ is and what He has already accomplished.

The trumpets, scroll, bowls, and beasts are not cryptic clues for predicting earthly disasters.

They are symbolic declarations of spiritual realities and Christ's triumph over sin and evil.

They uncover His judgment against apostasy and the establishment of His eternal Kingdom.

This heavenly reign is first revealed in Revelation chapters 4 and 5, which unveil a powerful moment directly following the resurrection of Jesus.

When John sees a door opened in heaven and is called to "come up hither," he is witnessing the heavenly realm receiving the risen Christ.

The Lamb that appears 'as it had been slain' is not a foreshadowing of future wrath but the risen Christ, newly glorified, standing in the heavenly court following His resurrection.

And the book does not end in destruction.

It concludes in glory.

The New Jerusalem descends.

God dwells with His people.

And the light of Christ illuminates all things (Revelation 21:3–23).

This is not a glimpse of a future hope.

It is a present reality for all who live in Him.

Peering Through the Fog: Interpreting Revelation Through the Right Lens

To fully understand Revelation, we must first examine the lenses through which it has been interpreted across history.

Our perspective shapes how we piece together its symbols and prophecies.

Among the most prominent interpretive frameworks are:

Futurism, Historicism, and Preterism—

Each offering a different timeline and theological foundation.

Futurism – Reading Revelation as Future Prophecy

Futurism sees Revelation as a detailed map of events still to come.

This view, widely embraced in modern evangelicalism, interprets the Beast, the Antichrist, the Great Tribulation, and the Mark of the Beast as literal, global events awaiting future fulfillment.

It predicts a final seven-year tribulation, a global dictator's rise, and Christ's eventual return to establish a physical millennial kingdom on earth.

Many books popularized this approach, often turning current headlines into prophetic clues.

But in doing so, they disconnect Revelation from its original audience and covenantal context.

Its meaning becomes ever-shifting, shaped by wars, elections, and disasters.

Additionally, futurist interpretations often apply a mixed hermeneutic—treating some symbols as literal and others as figurative without a consistent rationale.

For example, while the seven-headed, ten-horned beast is not to be taken literally, the New Jerusalem is interpreted as a literal future city descending from the sky. This inconsistency makes the message fragmented and difficult to grasp, often leaving readers unsure of which parts are symbolic, historical, or predictive.

This can leave believers trapped in a cycle of fear, constantly watching for signs of the end times.

Historicism – Revelation as a Panorama of Church History

Historicism interprets Revelation as a sweeping timeline of church history, stretching from the apostles to the Second Coming.

This view, held by many of the Reformers, sees the seven churches as representing distinct eras of church development.

Trumpets, seals, and bowls are linked to historical milestones such as the fall of Rome, the rise of Islam, and the Protestant Reformation.

While this perspective attempts to anchor Revelation in historical progression, its interpretations shift with each generation.

What one era sees as fulfillment, another reinterprets.

This speculative flexibility can obscure the central truth: Revelation is not primarily about history—it's about Jesus.

Preterism – Revelation as Fulfilled Prophecy

Preterism, from the Latin praeter (meaning "past"), reads Revelation as a prophecy already fulfilled, primarily in the first century.

It places the book within the covenantal change between the Old and New Covenants, focusing on the fall of Jerusalem in AD 70.

In this view:

The Beast and the Harlot represent apostate Jerusalem, not a physical, future one-world regime.

The Great Tribulation refers to the horrors of the Jewish-Roman War.

Christ's "coming" is a spiritual judgment marking the end of the Old Covenant age.

The New Jerusalem is not a far-off city, but the reality of the Church.

Preterism sees Revelation in its historical and covenantal setting, reminding us that God's promises in Christ have already been fulfilled.

Full Preterists and Partial Preterists are mainly distinguished by their view of Christ's future second coming.

Spiritual Preterism – The Lens of This Book

Spiritual Preterism emphasizes the fulfilled spiritual reign of Christ—less about political timelines, more about the unseen Kingdom within the hearts of His people.

This teaching goes deeper, emphasizing the spiritual realities now present through the victory secured at the cross.

Spiritual Preterism is not about political nations or global conspiracies.

It does not rely on charts, timelines, or speculative theories.

It centers entirely on Jesus.

It sees Revelation not as a countdown to the end, but as the actualization of a present spiritual kingdom.

When viewed through this lens, Revelation becomes a call to live boldly in the truth that He dismantled the dragon's dominion by truth and Spirit.

It liberates us from fear and invites us to see what so many have missed.

The Guiding Principle: Scripture Interprets Scripture

If the Scriptures are a tapestry woven across centuries, then Revelation is the completed masterpiece—the final unveiling of the glorious image God had promised all along.

It is the grand finale of a symphony composed through the Law, the Psalms, and the Prophets.

Revelation is not meant to stand in isolation.

As Peter wrote:

"No prophecy of the scripture is of any private interpretation." (2 Peter 1:20)

Every image in Revelation echoes something deeper, something familiar to the spiritually attentive.

Consider just a few:

The Lamb of Revelation 5 is symbolic of Christ and the Passover Lamb of Exodus—the one whose blood marked deliverance.

He is Isaiah's silent Lamb, led to the slaughter and exalted as Redeemer and King.

The scroll, sealed and awaiting revelation, mirrors the sealed visions of Daniel—now opened by the One found worthy, Christ alone.

The trumpets and bowls recall the plagues of Egypt, now expressed not as literal catastrophes, but as spiritual judgments against apostasy and covenantal rebellion.

The Beast, Dragon, and Harlot are not future dystopian villains—they are vivid symbols of spiritual opposition to Christ and His Church, centered in the rebellion of Old Covenant Jerusalem.

And the New Jerusalem? It is not a futuristic city in the clouds.

It is the fulfillment of Ezekiel's temple, Isaiah's city of righteousness, and Jeremiah's promise of a renewed people.

It is the Church—the radiant Bride of Christ, and the spiritual kingdom of God.

These are not isolated metaphors.

They are part of a divine pattern—threads woven from Genesis to Revelation pointing to Jesus.

Revelation doesn't break from Scripture—it completes it.

It draws from what was already spoken and fulfills what was long promised.

When we read Revelation through the lens of Scripture, its images stop confusing and start revealing.

They show us the truth now made manifest of Christ's reign, the beauty of His heavenly Bride, and the fulfillment of God's redemptive plan.

Revelation doesn't call us to speculate about tomorrow's headlines. It invites us to see, through a spiritual lens, the Kingdom already here—and the King already enthroned.

The Fulfillment of Prophecy: God's Plan Completed in Christ

Revelation is not a detached vision—it is the grand fulfillment of every prophecy, every promise, and every shadow that preceded it.

Consider the prophetic continuity across the ages:

(Genesis 3:15) The earliest prophecy of redemption speaks of a seed who would crush the serpent's head. In Revelation, that serpent, the great dragon, is cast down and defeated.

Having promised victory over the serpent in Eden, God revealed to Daniel the expanding dominion of the coming Son of Man.

(Daniel 7:13–14) Daniel beheld one like the Son of Man receiving dominion, glory, and a kingdom that would never pass away. Revelation shows that Son—Jesus—exalted, enthroned, and worshipped with eternal praise. (Revelation 5:12)

(Isaiah 65:17–19) Isaiah envisioned a new heavens and a new earth, where God would dwell with His people. In Revelation 21–22, that vision becomes reality in the New Jerusalem—the Church—God's redeemed people, where sorrow is no more and His presence abides forever.

(Ezekiel 47:1–12) Ezekiel saw a river flowing from the temple, bringing life wherever it went. Revelation echoes this image, revealing the river of life flowing from the throne of God and the Lamb, nourishing the people of Christ for all eternity.

(Jeremiah 31:31–34) The promise of a new covenant, written on hearts and marked by forgiveness, finds its ultimate expression in Revelation. The redeemed are sealed—not by law, but by the blood of the Lamb—forever His.

These prophecies are not waiting for some distant fulfillment.

They have already found their completion in Jesus.

Revelation doesn't draw us into dread of what might come—it invites us into the fullness of what has already arrived.

It is a kingdom already established,

A redemption already accomplished.

Conclusion: The Revelation of Christ's Fulfilled Victory

Revelation begins with its declaration:

"The Revelation of Jesus Christ." (Revelation 1:1)

Not the revelation of the Antichrist.

Not the prophecy of global catastrophe.

But the spiritual realities of Christ—His glory, His victory, and His fulfilled redemption.

When Jesus declared, "It is finished" (John 19:30), He wasn't speaking of a process to come.

He was announcing a kingdom established, a victory secured, a spiritual plan completed—not later, but now.

Revelation reveals and magnifies that glorious reality.

It doesn't look forward in fear, it looks inward and upward in faith.

This is not a coded enigma for the curious, it is a radiant proclamation for the faithful. As Paul declared, "For all the promises of God in him are yea, and in him Amen, unto the glory of God by us." (2 Corinthians 1:20)

"It is finished," was announcing a kingdom established—a masterpiece now revealed.

Key Takeaways:

Revelation is primarily an "unveiling" (apokalypsis) of Jesus Christ's triumph, not a cryptic forecast of future global calamities.

This interpretive lens, Spiritual Preterism, understands Revelation's prophecies as already fulfilled, emphasizing Christ's present spiritual reign and the indwelling Kingdom within believers.

The book aims to shift perspective from fear, speculation, and confusion to clarity, truth, and spiritual reality, seeing every symbol reflect Jesus and declare His victory.

Chapter 2

THE NEW JERUSALEM: CITY OF ETERNAL LIGHT

Awakening to the Radiant City Within: The Bride

What if the city, the New Jerusalem of Revelation 21 and 22, the one where peace never ends, perpetually radiant with the presence of God, was here now and spiritually woven into the fabric of our world?

In a creation marred by chaos, where kingdoms rise and fall and hopes are often dashed by the weight of darkness, Revelation unveils a reality more enduring than empires and more radiant than the sun: the New Jerusalem.

Here is the city of eternal light—a place where the glory of God illuminates every street and "the Lamb is the light thereof." It is the dwelling of God with His people, not confined to some distant age, but awakening now in hearts made new by Christ.

For this holy city is not built by human hands. It is the Bride adorned in splendor—the Church radiant in righteousness and the victorious people of God, living as citizens of heaven while still walking upon the earth. The reality of the New Jerusalem, not as brick and mortar, but as love, justice, and holiness made visible through those who bear His name.

In these pages, we will journey together into the heart of this divine vision, unveiling a city that is both the glorious culmination of God's redemptive story and the present reality into which we are now called to live.

A Note on Heaven and the New Jerusalem

Before we proceed, a crucial clarification is necessary. While this chapter argues that the New Jerusalem symbolizes the present covenantal reality of the Church, this does not negate the existence of heaven as the eternal hope of every believer. We live now as citizens of the kingdom, but we also await resurrection and the day we shall see Him face to face. The focus here is on the spiritual nature of the New Jerusalem as unveiled in Revelation, which is the Church alive today.

The New Jerusalem is manifest wherever believers live out His reign through justice, love, and mercy. It is not a dream deferred nor a distant future city. It is the now of God's Kingdom, alive in us, unfolding through us—His Bride, the living Church.

The Stone That Shattered Kingdoms: Daniel's Vision of the Coming Kingdom

Long before John saw the Holy City descending, the prophet Daniel saw a different vision—a statue representing the kingdoms of men: empires built on gold, silver, bronze, and iron. But then came a stone, cut without human hands, which struck the statue and shattered it into pieces. That stone became a mountain and filled the entire earth.

"Thou sawest till that a stone was cut out without hands, which smote the image upon his feet. And the stone that smote the image became a great mountain, and filled the whole earth." (Daniel 2:34–35)

This stone is Christ—and the mountain it becomes is His eternal Kingdom, growing not by force but by Spirit.

"And in the days of these kings shall the God of heaven set up a kingdom, which shall never be destroyed. It shall break in pieces and consume all these kingdoms, and it shall stand forever." (Daniel 2:44)

The New Jerusalem is the fulfillment of this prophecy. It is not the echo of an earthly empire—it is the unshakable mountain of God's kingdom, built without hands, rising not by force but by Spirit, and growing through lives surrendered to the Lamb.

In Daniel's day, the vision was mysterious. In John's day, it was unveiled. And in our day, it is reality.

The Perfect Dimensions: The New Jerusalem and the Holy of Holies

The New Jerusalem is the Holy of Holies—no longer confined to a temple, but spiritually present and vast, dwelling among God's people.

The cubical nature of its dimensions signifies the perfect dwelling place of God, not in a physical location but among His redeemed people.

John describes its astounding measurements:

"And the city lieth foursquare, and the length is as large as the breadth: and he measured the city with the reed, twelve thousand furlongs. The length and the breadth and the height of it are equal." (Revelation 21:16)

This description is not meant to be taken as a literal physical structure but as a symbol of divine perfection. The city is a perfect cube, mirroring the Holy of Holies in the Old Testament—the sacred space where God's presence dwelt.

"And the oracle in the forepart was twenty cubits in length, and twenty cubits in breadth, and twenty cubits in the height thereof: and he overlaid it with pure gold." (1 Kings 6:20)

The Holy of Holies in Solomon's Temple was also a perfect cube, signifying the dwelling of God among His people. Only the high priest could enter once a year, bearing the blood of atonement. But in the New Jerusalem, this sacred space is no longer restricted—God's presence is fully revealed, open to all who belong to Him.

"And I heard a great voice out of heaven saying, Behold, the tabernacle of God is with men, and he will dwell with them, and they shall be his people, and God himself shall be with them, and be their God." (Revelation 21:3)

This radical shift was made possible because Jesus, our great High Priest, has already entered the true Holy of Holies—not the earthly temple, but heaven itself—offering the final atoning sacrifice in His blood.

"But Christ being come a high priest of good things to come, by a greater and more perfect tabernacle, not made with hands, that is to say, not of this building; Neither by the blood of goats and calves, but by his own blood he entered in once into the holy place, having obtained eternal redemption for us." (Hebrews 9:11–12)

No longer does a high priest need to enter once a year, for Christ has done it once and for all, securing eternal access to the Father. The veil was torn (Matthew 27:51), the barrier removed, and now all who are in Christ dwell continually in His presence.

"Having therefore, brethren, boldness to enter into the holiest by the blood of Jesus, by a new and living way, which he hath consecrated for us, through the veil, that is to say, his flesh; And having an high priest over the house of God; Let us draw near with a true heart in full assurance of faith…" (Hebrews 10:19–22)

The New Jerusalem is not awaiting a future temple, for the true temple—the presence of God in Christ—has already been established. The Holy of Holies is no longer a chamber in a temple. It is now the Church itself—the dwelling place of the Spirit.

"And I saw no temple therein: for the Lord God Almighty and the Lamb are the temple of it." (Revelation 21:22)

The 12,000 furlongs that form the city's length, width, and height are not merely architectural details but a symbol of perfect completeness. In biblical numerology:

12 represents God's government—the twelve tribes of Israel, the twelve apostles, the twelve foundations.

1,000 represents divine fullness:

"A thousand years in thy sight are but as yesterday." (Psalm 90:4)

"For every beast of the forest is mine, and the cattle upon a thousand hills." — (Psalm 50:10)

Thus, 12,000 furlongs symbolize the fullness of God's perfect dwelling—a city that is not measured in physical miles but in the completeness of His presence.

Furthermore, the golden composition of both the Holy of Holies and the New Jerusalem emphasizes the divine nature of this dwelling place:

"And the city was pure gold, like unto clear glass." (Revelation 21:18)

This is not earthly gold but the purity and holiness of God's kingdom. Just as the high priest once entered the gold-covered Holy of Holies, now all who are in Christ dwell permanently in the presence of God, as His holy people.

The very idea of shadow becomes obsolete, eclipsed forever by the radiance of the Lamb.

"The city had no need of the sun, neither of the moon, to shine in it: for the glory of God did lighten it, and the Lamb is the light thereof." (Revelation 21:23)

This glory shines with heavenly radiance. This light is eternal, blazing with the brilliance of the One who spoke, "I am the Light of the World" (John 8:12). It is the glory of Christ, shining without dimming, filling every corner of the city, flooding every heart of its citizens.

To live as citizens of the New Jerusalem is to dwell in unending light. It means rejecting the shadows of sin and fear—casting off the veil of darkness and stepping fully into Christ's brilliance. As John reminds us, "If we walk in the light, as He is in the light, we have fellowship one with another, and the blood of Jesus Christ his Son cleanseth us from all sin." (1 John 1:7)

This is not a distant ideal but a lived reality under the risen Lamb.

The Bride Adorned: The Church as the New Jerusalem

She is not merely a city. She is a bride.

Arrayed in splendor, clothed in righteousness, and crowned with grace, the New Jerusalem descends like a bride prepared for her groom, not with jewels crafted by human hands, but adorned with the holiness of divine union.

This is no distant wedding awaiting a trumpet in the sky. The Church is the Bride even now. Her radiance is not deferred—it is visible in the love, righteousness, and faithfulness of those united to Christ.

Paul reveals this mystery in his letter to the Ephesians:

"Husbands, love your wives, even as Christ also loved the church, and gave himself for it; That he might sanctify and cleanse it with the washing of water by the word, That he might present it to himself a glorious church, not having spot, or wrinkle, or any such thing; but that it should be holy and without blemish." (Ephesians 5:25–27)

Then he unveils the true meaning behind this analogy:

"This is a great mystery: but I speak concerning Christ and the church." (Ephesians 5:32)

John reinforces this when the angel says:

"Come hither, I will shew thee the bride, the Lamb's wife." (Revelation 21:9)

And what does he show John? Not a woman in a white gown—but the New Jerusalem.

The Church is both the dwelling place and the beloved. She is the holy people made radiant through union with the Lamb.

"Let us be glad and rejoice, and give honour to him: for the marriage of the Lamb is come, and his wife hath made herself ready. And to her was granted that she should be arrayed in fine linen, clean, and white: for the fine linen is the righteousness of saints." (Revelation 19:7–8)

This righteousness is not earned—it is gifted. The garments of the Bride are woven from grace and obedience. Her beauty is not found in what she builds, but in who she has become: holy, set apart, radiant with the light of her Bridegroom.

The New Jerusalem has already descended. The Bride has already been adorned.

This is the Church's calling, not to wait passively for a someday ceremony, but to live now as a Bride and to reflect the love of Christ with every act of faithfulness. To echo the eternal vow written on the heart of every believer.

The Walls of Salvation and Gates of Praise: The Strength of the New Jerusalem

The New Jerusalem is the very structure of the redeemed people of God, built upon the foundation of Christ and His apostles. Isaiah prophesied of this city long before John's vision, declaring:

"Thou shalt call thy walls Salvation, and thy gates Praise" (Isaiah 60:18).

This prophecy of a city whose walls are Salvation and whose gates are Praise is directly connected to Jesus' proclamation in the synagogue. When Jesus stood and read from Isaiah 61:1–2, He declared:

"This day is this scripture fulfilled in your ears." (Luke 4:21)

The passage He read—Isaiah 61—flows directly from the prophecy of Isaiah 60, which describes the radiance and restoration of Zion, the New Jerusalem. There is no prophetic gap between them. Jesus was declaring the very fulfillment of the Kingdom and salvation that Isaiah had prophesied.

This means the New Jerusalem was not awaiting a future fulfillment but was already breaking into history through Christ's ministry. The walls of salvation had been established in Him. The gates of praise had been thrown open to welcome all who enter through the Lamb.

Isaiah foresaw that the New Jerusalem is encompassed by walls of salvation and entered through gates of praise. These are not lifeless stones and iron-bound doors, but the very fabric of the redeemed community—the Church, built upon the accomplished mission of Christ.

John, standing in awe of the heavenly vision, declares:

"And had a wall great and high, and had twelve gates, and at the gates twelve angels, and names written thereon, which are the names of the twelve tribes of the children of Israel." (Revelation 21:12)

These twelve gates stand as an everlasting testimony to the faithfulness of God, for through Israel the promise was given, and through Christ, it was fulfilled. Yet beyond the gates, beneath the very foundations of this holy city, another inscription is revealed:

"And the wall of the city had twelve foundations, and in them the names of the twelve apostles of the Lamb." (Revelation 21:14)

Here, the New Jerusalem is unmistakably identified as the Church, for its foundation is none other than the apostles of Christ, upon whom the Church was built. Paul confirms this truth in his letter to the Ephesians:

"Now therefore ye are no more strangers and foreigners, but fellowcitizens with the saints, and of the household of God; And are built upon the foundation of the apostles and prophets, Jesus Christ himself being the chief corner stone." (Ephesians 2:19–20)

What is this city, if not the dwelling place of God among His people? It is not a structure awaiting some distant fulfillment, but the very Body of Christ, standing upon the unshakable foundation of apostolic teaching and made radiant through the righteousness of the saints.

Isaiah's prophetic vision and John's heavenly revelation merge into one undeniable truth: The New Jerusalem is the Church, the Bride of Christ, already adorned and dwelling in the presence of her King. The walls of salvation and the gates of praise are not of brick and mortar but of the redeemed, standing secure in the sacrifice of Christ, lifting their voices in unending worship to the Lamb.

For those who enter through these gates, there is no fear, there is only the security of salvation and the joy of eternal praise.

The Living Foundations of the New Jerusalem: Built on Christ, Adorned in Glory

The apostles were not merely followers of Christ; they were the chosen instruments through whom the Church was established. Their names, etched into the very foundations of the New Jerusalem, signify the eternal nature of the Kingdom they proclaimed. But what holds these foundations together? It is none other than Jesus Christ Himself—the chief cornerstone upon which the entire structure stands.

"Behold, I lay in Zion a chief corner stone, elect, precious: and he that believeth on him shall not be confounded." (1 Peter 2:6)

What John sees in Revelation is not merely a symbolic tribute to the apostles but a declaration that the Church, built upon their testimony, is the New Jerusalem itself. This city does not rest on human wisdom or earthly power but upon the everlasting gospel that was first entrusted to those twelve men.

Yet John's vision goes deeper still, revealing that these foundations are not bare stones, but adorned with radiant gemstones:

"And the foundations of the wall of the city were garnished with all manner of precious stones. The first foundation was jasper; the second, sapphire; the third, a chalcedony; the fourth, an emerald;

The fifth, sardonyx; the sixth, sardius; the seventh, chrysolite; the eighth, beryl; the ninth, a topaz; the tenth, a chrysoprasus; the eleventh, a jacinth; the twelfth, an amethyst." (Revelation 21:19–20)

Each stone, with its unique brilliance, reflects the glory of the divine work accomplished through the apostles. Just as their lives bore witness to Christ, so too does the radiance of these foundations declare the beauty of the Church, purified, and adorned for her King.

This imagery finds a striking parallel in the Old Testament, where the high priest of Israel bore a breastplate set with twelve precious stones, each engraved with the name of one of the twelve tribes. (Exodus 28:17–21)

The high priest bore these names in divine intercession—a foreshadowing of the eternal covenant.

Now, in the New Jerusalem, the twelve apostles—whose names are inscribed upon the foundations—serve as the eternal testimony of the new and better covenant, established in Christ.

Thus, the New Jerusalem stands as a city not merely built of stone and light but as a living testament to the redemptive work of God. Its walls declare salvation. Its gates resound with praise. Its foundations shine with the eternal glory of Christ, the apostles, and the Church—the Bride who has made herself ready.

For those who stand upon this foundation, there is no fear of collapse, no shifting ground, no uncertain future. The city stands forever, upheld by the unshakable rock of Christ and adorned with the beauty of His unchanging truth.

A Kingdom of Peace and Restoration: Sin Causes Spiritual Death

What does it mean to live in a kingdom where sorrow has no home?

In the New Jerusalem, the griefs of Earth are exiled forever. There, we hear the promise spoken from the very throne of God:

"And God shall wipe away all tears from their eyes; and there shall be no more death, neither sorrow, nor crying, neither shall there be any more pain: for the former things are passed away." (Revelation 21:4)

Christ did not come simply to promise peace; He came to be our peace.

"Peace I leave with you, my peace I give unto you: not as the world giveth, give I unto you." (John 14:27)

Yet to understand the fullness of this peace, we must remember the cause of sorrow and death: sin itself.

From the very beginning, Scripture teaches that sin is not merely a mistake—it is death working its way into the soul.

"The soul that sinneth, it shall die." (Ezekiel 18:4)

"For the wages of sin is death; but the gift of God is eternal life through Jesus Christ our Lord." (Romans 6:2)

The death Christ conquered is not merely physical death, but spiritual death—the separation from God brought on by sin. It was sin that introduced the sting of death into the world.

But now, through the accomplished work of Christ, the sting has been removed, the curse broken, and the victory secured:

"O death, where is thy sting? O grave, where is thy victory? The sting of death is sin. But thanks be to God, which giveth us the victory through our Lord Jesus Christ." (1 Corinthians 15:55)

This is the heartbeat of the New Jerusalem.

A people who carry the peace of Christ into a restless world. A kingdom where the curse has been lifted, the separation healed, and the sting of death destroyed. A holy city whose gates are never shut because fear has been banished, sin has been conquered, and love rules without rival.

Here, in the New Jerusalem, there is no more death—not the ending of physical life, but the end of spiritual separation, the restoration of perfect union between God and His people.

The death that sin once demanded has been swallowed up by the life Christ freely gives.

The Kingdom Is Now: Rejecting a Distant Hope

"Again, the kingdom of heaven is like unto treasure hid in a field; the which when a man hath found, he hideth, and for joy thereof goeth and selleth all that he hath, and buyeth that field." (Matthew 13:4)

The New Jerusalem is not waiting for some final trumpet blast to unfold. It is already in spiritual view. It is already alive in the hearts of those who confess that Jesus is Lord.

"The time is fulfilled, and the Kingdom of God is at hand..." (Mark 1:1)

This was Christ's declaration—not as a distant prophecy, but as a present reality. He came to bring the Kingdom near. He came to inaugurate a Kingdom that would grow like leaven in the dough, like seed in the soil, like light breaking into the night.

To relegate the New Jerusalem to some far-off era is to overlook the holy streets taking shape in acts of forgiveness, in communities of grace, in churches ablaze with the love of Christ.

Yes, there is a heaven we have not yet seen.

But make no mistake: the Kingdom has already broken into the world, and the New Jerusalem is already built in the lives of those who choose faith over fear, love over lawlessness, and surrender over self.

The New Jerusalem is not a place you will one day enter.

It is a reality you are always invited to embody—right here, right now, in this very moment.

So, step into the city.

Walk its golden streets wherever you go.

Let its walls of salvation surround you.

Let its light radiate from within you.

Be filled with gates of praise.

Citizens of the Eternal City: Living Out the New Jerusalem

To belong to the New Jerusalem is not merely to believe in its existence.

It is to embody its essence.

It is to awaken each morning beneath the banner of a Kingdom that cannot be shaken and to walk through this world as ambassadors of the eternal city whose gates never close.

"For our citizenship is in heaven." (Philippians 3:20)

These are not poetic words for someday. They are the truest description of who we are now—a people set apart, living by the values of the city that has already descended, radiant in the light of the Lamb.

And if we are its citizens, then we are its architects, too—laying its foundations with every choice to love our neighbor, every act of compassion toward the forgotten, every moment we dare to bring heaven's hope into earth's ache.

This is the calling of the redeemed.

For the holy city is not built by human hands.

It rises wherever the people of God refuse to bow to the lesser kingdoms of this age.

It advances with every surrendered life, every humble servant, every courageous act of love.

And the question is not if the New Jerusalem is here, but will we, through salvation, enter it?

Walking as Kings: Living in the Glory of the New Jerusalem

The New Jerusalem is not only the dwelling place of God; it is the place of kings. And you are one of them.

Revelation opens with this powerful declaration:

"And hath made us kings and priests unto God and his Father; to him be glory and dominion for ever and ever. Amen." (Revelation 1:6)

We are not merely forgiven—we are enthroned. Christ has not only redeemed us; He has crowned us.

"And hath raised us up together, and made us sit together in heavenly places in Christ Jesus." (Ephesians 2:6) We are citizens of heaven, yes— but also rulers in His spiritual Kingdom, called to walk in divine authority and holy purpose.

Jesus, the King of kings, wears many crowns:

"And on His head were many crowns." (Revelation 19:12)

And He reigns not as an earthly monarch, but as the eternal Lord over a spiritual kingdom.

When Pilate asked Him if He was a king, Jesus answered with eternal clarity:

"Thou sayest that I am a king. To this end was I born, and for this cause came I into the world." (John 18:37)

"My kingdom is not of this world." (John 18:36)

This is the Kingdom of the New Jerusalem—not built with human hands, not adorned with fading gold, but radiant with the glory of the Lamb.

To see Jesus crowned, you must see with spiritual eyes.

His royalty was veiled to the world. He bore no golden scepter, no robe of silk. And yet, He wore many spiritual crowns. Likewise, you are a king in His Kingdom, even if the world does not see your crown.

"And hast made us unto our God kings and priests: and we shall reign on the earth." (Revelation 5:10)

This is a now inheritance. This reign has already begun.

Revelation testifies that the redeemed already walk in the city's light, offering glory not to themselves, but to the Lamb:

"And the nations of them which are saved shall walk in the light of it: and the kings of the earth do bring their glory and honour into it."

Who are these kings? They are not the proud of the earth, but the redeemed—the ones who have bowed to the Lamb, been washed in His blood, and now walk in His light. They are you.

The world may not see your crown, but heaven does. The city may not have walls of stone, but it has gates wide open to every king who walks in the light of the Lamb.

And what of the golden streets?

Too often, they are seen as a future luxury—as if God were obsessed with wealth. But Revelation declares:

"And the street of the city was pure gold, as it were transparent glass." (Revelation 21:2)

Though not with physical feet, the Christian walks these golden streets even now—spiritually, by faith, through obedience to the Lamb. The golden streets represent spiritual victory, heavenly authority, and the path of righteousness laid out for those who belong to the Lamb.

A thousand years of walking on physical gold would hold no eternal meaning. But to walk in the Spirit—to live daily in holiness, truth, and love—that is the real path through the city.

See the gold with spiritual eyes.

See the crowns with spiritual vision.

See the Kingdom as a present inheritance.

For the kings of the earth are already walking its streets. The saved are already bringing their glory into the city.

And the Lamb is its light.

The River and the Tree of Life: Ezekiel's Vision Fulfilled in the New Jerusalem

Flowing from the very heart of the New Jerusalem, from the throne of God and of the Lamb, is a river unlike any this world has ever known. Crystal clear, unceasing, alive with holiness, this river does not simply quench thirst—it awakens life.

"And he shewed me a pure river of water of life, clear as crystal, proceeding out of the throne of God and of the Lamb. In the midst of the street of it, and on either side of the river, was there the tree of life, which bare twelve manner of fruits, and yielded her fruit every month: and the leaves of the tree were for the healing of the nations." (Revelation 22:1–2)

This breathtaking vision is not new—it echoes a prophecy given centuries earlier. The prophet Ezekiel also saw a river flowing from the temple of God, bringing life to all it touched.

"Then said he unto me, These waters issue out toward the east country, and go down into the desert, and go into the sea: which being brought forth into the sea, the waters shall be healed. And it shall come to pass, that every thing that liveth, which moveth, whithersoever the rivers shall come, shall live...

And by the river upon the bank thereof, on this side and on that side, shall grow all trees for meat, whose leaf shall not fade, neither shall the fruit thereof be consumed: it shall bring forth new fruit according to his months, because their waters they issued out of the sanctuary: and the fruit thereof shall be for meat, and the leaf thereof for medicine." (Ezekiel 47:8–9, 12)

Ezekiel's vision, once shrouded in mystery, is now fully unveiled. The river that once flowed from the temple in his vision now flows from the throne of God and the Lamb. The trees bearing fruit for healing are no longer distant symbols but present realities in the New Jerusalem—the dwelling of God among His people.

Jesus Himself spoke of this river, revealing its spiritual nature:

"If any man thirst, let him come unto Me, and drink. He that believeth on Me… out of his belly shall flow rivers of living water." (John 7:37–38)

This river is the Spirit of God, flowing through His people, bringing life to a world still caught in spiritual drought. The Tree of Life, once barred by the flaming sword in Eden, now flourishes freely, its fruit abundant, its leaves healing the nations. The curse is lifted, and the people of God are sustained in His presence.

"And there shall be no more curse: but the throne of God and of the Lamb shall be in it; and his servants shall serve him." (Revelation 22:3)

This is not a distant hope. It is a radiant now—alive, present, and transforming. Even now, the Spirit flows within the Church. The leaves of the Tree of Life are bringing restoration to all who enter the gates of the Kingdom.

Conclusion: Walking in the Light of the New Jerusalem

This is the mystery unveiled in Revelation: the New Jerusalem is not only the final chapter of redemption's story—it is the present reality of the people of God, already risen from the rubble of a broken world. It is the Kingdom come, the city of eternal light, here and now, alive in the hearts of those who belong to the Lamb.

And so, beloved, hear the call:

Live as citizens of the city that cannot fall.

Carry its light into every shadowed place.

Pour its living water into every parched soul.

Bear its fruit until the world tastes and sees that the Lord is good.

For the New Jerusalem is not an idle dream, nor a hope deferred.

The city has descended.

It is the Church awakened.

It is you. It is us. It is now.

And let the world see, through your life, the beauty of the New Jerusalem.

The writer of Hebrews affirms this present spiritual truth with unmistakable clarity:

"But ye are come unto mount Sion, and unto the city of the living God, the heavenly Jerusalem, and to an innumerable company of angels, to the general assembly and church of the firstborn, which are written in heaven, and to God the Judge of all, and to the spirits of just men made perfect, and to Jesus the mediator of the new covenant." (Hebrews 12:22–24)

Key Takeaways:

The New Jerusalem is not a literal future city descending from the sky, but the spiritual reality of the Church—the Bride of Christ—alive and manifest today.

Its perfect, cubical dimensions mirror the Holy of Holies, signifying God's dwelling place is now among His redeemed people through Christ, making His presence fully accessible to all believers.

Living as citizens of the New Jerusalem means walking in unending spiritual light, rejecting the shadows of sin, and embodying Christ's reign through justice, love, and mercy today.

Chapter 3

MYSTERY BABYLON: BEYOND THE HARLOT'S VEIL

The Harlot's Seduction: A Call to Discernment and Faithfulness

In the vast and intricate tapestry of biblical symbolism, few figures cast a shadow as mysterious and provocative as Mystery Babylon—the great harlot of Revelation 17.

Clothed in splendor, holding a golden cup of abominations, and seated upon many waters, she stands as a sobering portrait of spiritual betrayal, intoxicating the nations with her unfaithfulness and presiding over the blood of prophets and saints.

Her beauty is deceptive, her riches stained with blood.

But to rightly discern her, we must not only trace her symbols—we must listen for the cry of the prophets echoing across time.

Who is this enigmatic woman? What story does she tell, and why does her downfall resound so profoundly within John's apocalyptic vision?

In these pages, we will journey into the depths of this symbol, examining the scriptural evidence that Mystery Babylon represents not some distant empire, but spiritual apostate Jerusalem itself—the city previously set apart to bear God's name, yet tragically given over to idolatry, violence, and the rejection of her Messiah.

The Tragedy and Triumph: Judgment and Restoration

This realization is sobering. To see the beloved city unveiled in judgment stirs a grief mingled with awe, reminding us that God's call to faithfulness has always been a call of love.

And yet, this is not merely a study of ancient prophecy or historical judgment. The harlot's fall is a timeless warning—a divine summons to every generation to guard against the seduction of compromise, to resist the allure of corrupted religion, and to remain faithful to the Lamb.

By unfolding the rich layers of Revelation's imagery, we will seek not only to identify Mystery Babylon but to confront her within ourselves, wherever pride replaces humility, ritual replaces relationship, and power eclipses purity. In doing so, we will rediscover the hope that lies beyond her ruin: the radiant vision of the New Jerusalem, the faithful Bride, and the eternal Kingdom of God.

A Veiled Betrayal Unmasked: The Harlot and the True City

The vision of Mystery Babylon unfolds with haunting grandeur as it draws us into the scene:

"And there came one of the seven angels which had the seven vials, and talked with me, saying unto me, Come hither; I will shew unto thee the judgment of the great whore that sitteth upon many waters." (Revelation 17:1)

Here, John is summoned to behold the harlot's fate—a figure whose power stretches far beyond a single place or people. She sits upon "many waters," a cryptic detail that begs for interpretation. What are these waters, and why is her influence so vast?

Thankfully, Revelation itself provides the key. A few verses later, the mystery begins to dissolve:

"And he saith unto me, The waters which thou sawest, where the whore sitteth, are peoples, and multitudes, and nations, and tongues. (Revelation 17:15)

In this, we see that Babylon's dominion is not confined to geography. Her reach is spiritual, cultural, and global. She intoxicates the nations through seductive influence, drawing the hearts of kings and the souls of people into her unfaithfulness.

To understand the gravity of this symbolism, we must look backward, to the prophets of old. Jeremiah 51:12–13 echoes through the ages with eerie familiarity:

"O thou that dwellest upon many waters, abundant in treasures, thine end is come, and the measure of thy covetousness."

These words, first spoken over ancient Babylon, resonate anew in John's vision. The "many waters" of Jeremiah referred to Babylon's strategic position along the Euphrates—a city enriched by trade and power, yet destined for divine judgment. In Revelation, the same language is repurposed, this time pointing us to a new Babylon, clothed not just in wealth, but in spiritual adultery.

And here, the parallels deepen. As ancient Babylon fell under the weight of its pride, violence, and idolatry, so too does Mystery Babylon stand condemned. Yet the prophetic spotlight shifts from the physical empire of old to a greater, more personal warning.

At the heart of John's vision is not merely a portrait of a city's fall—but a cautionary tale for all who would seek security in anything other than the Lamb.

The Adornment of Apostasy: A Crowned and Bejeweled Betrayal

Mystery Babylon symbolizes apostate Jerusalem due to her covenant-breaking and spiritual adultery, vividly prophesied by Old Testament prophets.

The imagery of the harlot, Mystery Babylon, is drawn directly from the prophetic indictments of Jerusalem's unfaithfulness in Ezekiel 16 and 23.

Mystery Babylon, in this context, is none other than first-century apostate Jerusalem—once adorned in covenant, now unveiled in judgment.

Once adorned by God with fine linens and precious stones, Jerusalem turned those blessings into instruments of spiritual adultery.

John echoes this vividly: the harlot is dressed in purple and scarlet, adorned with gold and jewels—symbols of corrupted holiness.

Just as the high priest bore stones for intercession, the harlot wears them in betrayal.

The comparison is deliberate and sobering.

This spiritual unfaithfulness, masked in splendor, is the heart of Babylon's judgment.

"With whom the kings of the earth committed fornication, and the inhabitants of the earth were made drunk with the wine of her fornication."

This is not new language for the people of God. The prophets had long used such imagery to describe a tragedy far deeper than mere political rebellion—the betrayal of covenant love. Nowhere is this more powerfully expressed than in Ezekiel 16, where God commands the prophet:

"Son of man, cause Jerusalem to know her abominations." (Ezekiel 16:2)

Jerusalem, once chosen and adorned by God, is depicted as a cherished bride who turned away from her first love. Trusting in her own beauty and prosperity, she sought alliances with the surrounding nations, indulging in idolatry and forsaking the One who had rescued and exalted her. Ezekiel's vision is unflinching—Jerusalem, once cherished, had become so deeply entangled in spiritual infidelity that restoration seemed impossible.

The parallels to Babylon in Revelation are unmistakable.

Ezekiel 16:15 speaks of Jerusalem's pride in her beauty.

Verse 26 describes her lustful alliances with Egypt.

Verse 28 names her insatiable longing for Assyria.

Verse 29 mourns her endless thirst for more lovers.

Verse 32 declares her an adulterous wife, spurning faithfulness.

And as if this indictment were not severe enough, Ezekiel 23 deepens the narrative. There we meet Aholibah, a symbolic representation of Jerusalem herself. Her transgressions surpass even those of her sister, Samaria. Her "inordinate love" and graphic unfaithfulness reveal a people not merely sinning in ignorance but actively embracing corruption. The spiritual harlotry of Jerusalem was not hidden—it was flaunted.

John's vision of the harlot in Revelation is not an isolated invention. It is the prophetic tradition brought to its final, climactic expression. The same city once rebuked by Ezekiel now reemerges as the great harlot, arrayed with outward holiness masking inward corruption, seducing the nations and intoxicated by her own treachery.

Her wine of fornication is more than the indulgence of idols. It is the total abandonment of covenant faithfulness—the persistent trading of divine glory for the fleeting promises of political power, wealth, and security. Time and again, Jerusalem turned from the living God to the gods of her neighbors, forgetting that her beauty was given, her splendor bestowed, and her purpose holy.

The message reverberates across the ages: whenever God's people forsake their calling, trusting in the systems of the world over the faithfulness of their King, the spirit of Babylon arises. And the words of the prophets find their mark once again, urging us to remember that spiritual unfaithfulness, no matter how well-disguised in religious garb, leads only to judgment and ruin.

The Outward Not Inward Beauty: How Beauty Became Betrayal

The image of Mystery Babylon grows ever more striking as John describes her appearance:

"And the woman was arrayed in purple and scarlet colour, and decked with gold and precious stones and pearls, having a golden cup in her hand full of abominations and filthiness of her fornication." (Revelation 17:4)

It is a vision of lavish beauty and wealth, yet beneath the dazzling exterior lies corruption of the deepest kind. Her splendor is not the glory of holiness, but the seductive allure of spiritual infidelity. The symbols John uses here are not random—they are deeply rooted in the language of the prophets and the imagery of the temple itself.

Ezekiel 16 offers the clearest parallel. There, Jerusalem is portrayed as a beloved bride, adorned by God Himself with the finest garments and jewelry:

"I decked thee also with ornaments, and I put bracelets upon thy hands, and a chain on thy neck. And I put a jewel on thy forehead, and earrings in thine ears, and a beautiful crown upon thine head. Thus wast thou decked with gold and silver; and thy raiment was of fine linen, and silk, and broidered work; thou didst eat fine flour, and honey, and oil: and thou wast exceeding beautiful, and thou didst prosper into a kingdom." (Ezekiel 16:11–13)

But beauty became her downfall. What had been given as a sign of covenant love was prostituted for the approval of foreign gods and earthly powers. Just as Jerusalem was once clothed in divine favor and fell into unfaithfulness, so too does the harlot of Revelation glitter with stolen glory, her outward majesty masking her inner decay.

John's description of the harlot's adornments is rich with temple symbolism. Gold and precious stones recall the splendor of Solomon's temple (1 Kings 6:20–22) and the sacred breastplate of the High Priest (Exodus 28:17–20). These were the very materials that once reflected the holiness of God's presence among His people. Now, in the vision of Babylon, these same treasures are twisted into emblems of arrogance, idolatry, and spiritual prostitution.

Even the mention of pearls, while not part of the temple's historical decor, carries deep symbolic weight. In Revelation 21:21 pearls appear again— not on the harlot, but as the gates of the New Jerusalem, the pure and eternal dwelling place of God with His people. The contrast is deliberate. What the harlot uses to decorate herself in false glory, the Bride of Christ receives as an eternal inheritance of righteousness.

The message is sobering: the very blessings once bestowed upon Jerusalem became instruments of her seduction. Her chosen status did not guard her from downfall. Instead, the gifts intended to glorify God were used to glorify herself, and her unfaithfulness led to her ruin.

Ancient Babylon fell beneath the weight of its pride and idolatry. Likewise, Jerusalem—though chosen—abandoned her covenant. And so, the language of fornication, harlotry, and abominations becomes the fitting indictment of a city that forgot her first love.

But Revelation's harlot is not only a spiritual figure. She is a mirror held up to the people of God in every age. When we take the gifts of God and use them for self-promotion, when we trade covenant intimacy for worldly acclaim, we, too, echo the story of Babylon. And the call resounds across time: return to faithfulness, lest beauty become ruin and blessing turn to judgment.

The New Jerusalem: The Inheritance of the Faithful

The fall of the harlot is not the end of the story. In the divine drama of Revelation, judgment is never the final word. Out of the ashes of apostasy, from the ruins of unfaithfulness, arises a vision of breathtaking beauty: the New Jerusalem, the Kingdom of God, as explained in the previous chapter.

Where the harlot was clothed in purple and scarlet, flaunting stolen glory and drunken on the blood of the righteous, the Bride shines with purity, clothed not in garments of excess, but in the radiant splendor of holiness. Where Babylon seduced the nations with her abominations, the New Jerusalem invites the nations to healing, to peace, to the unbroken presence of God.

This new city stands as the eternal antithesis of the old, apostate Jerusalem. No longer marked by betrayal, idolatry, and bloodshed, this Jerusalem descends from heaven as the fulfillment of all God's promises—a people purified, a community redeemed, a kingdom established not on power or pride, but on the faithfulness of the Lamb.

And so, the golden cup held by the harlot becomes more than just a symbol of judgment. It is a closing chapter—the final reckoning for covenant unfaithfulness. In her fall, the old order of things passes away. The age of temple sacrifices, national privilege, and legalistic striving ends. In its place rises the new covenant, written on the hearts of a people drawn from every tribe, tongue, and nation, united in Christ.

Here, both Jew and Gentile find their inheritance—not in a physical city built by human hands, but in the heavenly Jerusalem, where God dwells among His people forever. No more tears. No more death. No more night.

The harlot's story is a cautionary tale, but the Bride's story is our hope. For even as Babylon falls, the gates of the New Jerusalem stand open wide, welcoming all who thirst for righteousness into the eternal embrace of the Kingdom that cannot be shaken.

The Double Measure of Justice: Repaying Babylon's Iniquity

Within the unfolding judgment of Mystery Babylon, we encounter a divine principle as ancient as the prophets and as sobering as the apocalypse itself: double retribution. Revelation 18:6 pronounces this unflinching decree:

"Reward her even as she rewarded you, and double unto her double according to her works: in the cup which she hath filled fill to her double."

Here, justice is not arbitrary or reactionary. It is measured, deliberate, and complete—reflecting the severity of Babylon's crimes with an equal, and doubled, response. This is no innovation of John's vision. The roots of this judgment are deeply planted in the soil of Israel's prophetic tradition, where God's justice is portrayed as perfectly proportionate to the rebellion it confronts.

Jeremiah 16:18 declares:

"And first I will recompense their iniquity and their sin double; because they have defiled my land, they have filled mine inheritance with the carcases of their detestable and abominable things."

Here, the judgment upon Israel is not merely punitive—it is revealing. The defilement of God's holy inheritance demanded not just correction, but a retribution that matched the depth of the corruption. The land itself cried out for cleansing. The sin was severe; the response was thorough.

Similarly, Isaiah 40:2 proclaims:

"Speak ye comfortably to Jerusalem, and cry unto her, that her warfare is accomplished, that her iniquity is pardoned: for she hath received of the Lord's hand double for all her sins."

In this, we glimpse not only the finality of judgment but also the hope that follows it. Double retribution is not the end of God's story. It clears the way for comfort, restoration, and new beginnings. What is fully judged can also be fully healed.

This is the rhythm of Revelation.

The symbolism is precise. Just as Jeremiah 51:7 describes ancient Babylon as:

"A golden cup in the Lord's hand, making all the earth drunk,"

so too does apostate Jerusalem—the new Babylon of John's vision—become the vessel through which corruption spreads, seducing the nations and defiling the sacred. But the cup she filled with sin is the same cup from which she must now drink. And she will drink it double.

This is divine justice: exact, complete, and redemptive in its purpose. The punishment mirrors the crime, not out of vengeance, but to reveal the full weight of sin and the absolute necessity of cleansing. God's double retribution ensures that evil exhausts itself, leaving no residue to poison the holy city that will soon descend from heaven.

For us, the principle of double retribution is more than ancient prophecy or apocalyptic imagery. It stands as a stark reminder that spiritual infidelity has real consequences. When covenant people exchange truth for falsehood, purity for compromise, worship for idolatry, there is always a reckoning.

Yet, embedded within this principle is also the promise that judgment leads to restoration. God's justice clears the path for mercy. His reckoning makes way for renewal. But we must be vigilant. The same dangers that seduced Jerusalem lurk in every age. The spirit of Babylon whispers still.

So let us live as a people who remember:

That sin, left unchecked, multiplies.

That judgment, when it comes, is not unjust.

And that beyond discipline lies a city whose gates never close, where righteousness dwells forever.

The cup of Babylon is full. But the river of life flows freely for those who turn from her ways and embrace the way of the New Jerusalem.

The Blood of the Prophets: Jerusalem's Long Betrayal

The contrast between the Bride and the Harlot becomes even more vivid when we remember the tragic legacy of ancient Jerusalem.

Rather than being a faithful light to the nations, the city that once housed the presence of God became the graveyard of His messengers. Jesus Himself mourned over her, crying out:

"O Jerusalem, Jerusalem, thou that killest the prophets, and stonest them which are sent unto thee!" (Matthew 23:37)

Instead of receiving the words of correction and repentance, Jerusalem silenced the very voices sent to save her. The prophets were not honored within her gates—they were hunted.

As Jesus declared:

"Nevertheless I must walk to day, and tomorrow, and the day following: for it cannot be that a prophet perish out of Jerusalem." (Luke 13:33)

This deep-rooted betrayal culminated in the rejection and crucifixion of Christ Himself—the ultimate Prophet, the fulfillment of every covenant promise.

Thus, when Revelation unveils the harlot adorned in stolen glory and drunken with "the blood of the prophets, and of saints," it is not a foreign city it describes—it is the very city that had once been chosen, now fallen through unfaithfulness.

Mystery Babylon is not a symbol of general evil—it is a solemn indictment of apostate Jerusalem, the city that killed the prophets, betrayed the covenant, and refused her King.

In contrast, the New Jerusalem—the Bride of Christ—is a city built not on rejection, but on reception.

She does not shed the blood of the righteous; she is redeemed by it.

She does not stone the prophets; she lives by their Spirit and testimony.

The New Jerusalem embodies faithfulness, purity, and covenant loyalty.

Where the old city was condemned for her betrayal, the New Jerusalem shines as the radiant fulfillment of all God's promises—faithful, fruitful, and forever united with the Lamb.

The Rejected Son and the Transferred Kingdom: Jesus' Parable of the Landowner

As Jesus approached the final days of His earthly ministry, He spoke a piercing parable that laid bare the unfolding tragedy of Jerusalem and foreshadowed the very judgment John would later witness in Revelation.

"Hear another parable: There was a certain householder, which planted a vineyard, and hedged it round about... and let it out to husbandmen, and went into a far country." (Matthew 21:33)

In this parable, the landowner represents God, and the vineyard is Israel. The tenants—those entrusted with its care—are the religious leaders of Jerusalem. When the time of harvest came, they refused to render the fruits. They beat, stoned, and killed the servants sent to them—representing the long line of prophets God sent throughout the generations. Finally, the landowner sends his own son, saying, "They will reverence my son." But instead, they cast him out and slew him.

This is no generic moral tale. It is a divine indictment.

Jesus then asks, "When the lord therefore of the vineyard cometh, what will he do unto those husbandmen?" The crowd responds: "He will miserably destroy those wicked men, and will let out his vineyard unto other husbandmen, which shall render him the fruits in their seasons." (Matthew 21:41)

Here, Jesus unveils the divine consequence of Jerusalem's long betrayal—the very theme echoed in Revelation 17 and 18. The old covenant caretakers who rejected the prophets and killed the Son would be cast out. The vineyard—the Kingdom—would be given to others. As Jesus declared:

"Therefore say I unto you, The kingdom of God shall be taken from you, and given to a nation bringing forth the fruits thereof." (Matthew 21:43)

This is not just a rebuke of the Sanhedrin—it is the prophetic disclosure of a spiritual transfer: from the apostate Jerusalem, now become the harlot, to the New Jerusalem, the Bride.

The whore of Revelation rejected the Son.

The Bride receives Him with joy.

The old city killed the prophets and cast out their Messiah.

The new city is built upon the foundation of the apostles and prophets, Jesus Christ Himself being the chief cornerstone (Ephesians 2:20).

The tenants were entrusted with a spiritual inheritance but failed to bear fruit. So the Kingdom was given to a people—Jew and Gentile—united in Christ, who would yield the fruit of the Spirit.

The parable is thus a spiritual hinge—a divine echo across the Gospel and Revelation. It connects the harlot's judgment to the Bride's vindication.

The landowner has come.

The Son has been slain.

And the vineyard now belongs to the Bride who bears fruit in His name.

Harlot: Reinforcing the Identity of the Whore

One of the most striking confirmations of Mystery Babylon's identity emerges through the subtle yet profound parallels between the treasures mourned at her fall and the sacred objects once used in Jerusalem's Temple worship. These connections are no coincidence. They serve to draw a devastating contrast between the city's holy calling and its eventual descent into spiritual corruption.

What was once consecrated to God's glory has now become the attire of a harlot. The same elements that once adorned the sanctuary are paraded in the streets of Babylon, no longer symbols of worship, but trophies of seduction and excess. Through these parallels, John masterfully reveals that apostate Jerusalem, now intoxicated with idolatry and injustice, has become the very embodiment of the harlot.

The identity of Mystery Babylon as apostate Jerusalem is powerfully reinforced when we compare the 'merchandise' mourned at her fall (Revelation 18) with the sacred items of the Temple. This is not a random trade manifest; it is a spiritual inventory of sacredness profaned, item by item.

"And the merchants of the earth shall weep and mourn over her; for no man buyeth their merchandise any more:

The merchandise of gold, and silver, and precious stones, and of pearls, and fine linen, and purple, and silk, and scarlet, and all thyine wood, and all manner vessels of ivory, and all manner vessels of most precious wood, and of brass, and iron, and marble,

And cinnamon, and odours, and ointments, and frankincense, and wine, and oil, and fine flour, and wheat, and beasts, and sheep, and horses, and chariots, and slaves, and souls of men." (Revelation 18:11–13)

Gold, Silver, and Precious Stones

Jerusalem's Temple radiated with gold and silver, adorned with precious stones and craftsmanship dedicated to the glory of God. The Ark of the Covenant, the Menorah, and the High Priest's breastplate sparkled with sacred purpose (Exodus 25–28). Yet, in Revelation 17:4, the harlot wears these same elements, no longer as emblems of holiness but as ornaments of self-exaltation. What was meant for worship now becomes bait for seduction, signaling Jerusalem's moral and spiritual collapse.

Fine Linen, Purple, Silk, and Scarlet

Once reserved for the High Priest's garments and the curtains of the Holy Place (Exodus 28:5–8), these fabrics represented purity and priestly honor. But now, the harlot drapes herself in these same colors—not to minister before the Lord, but to advertise her infidelity to the nations. Sacred beauty, twisted into the costume of betrayal.

Thyine Wood, Ivory, Brass, Iron, and Marble

These rare materials, once fashioned into the Temple's sacred vessels and holy furnishings (1 Kings 6:15–20), now appear on the trade manifest of Babylon, reduced to mere commodities. Jerusalem's spiritual heritage is auctioned off, her sanctity commercialized, her purpose profaned.

Cinnamon, Odours, Ointments, and Frankincense

Once lifted as fragrant offerings on the altar (Exodus 30:34–38), these spices now perfume the harlot's chambers, their sacred aroma diluted by indulgence and greed. The sweet incense meant for the worship of God has become the scent of spiritual adultery.

Wine and Oil

These were the staples of sacrifice and anointing (Leviticus 2:1–16), poured out in worship. But in Babylon's fall, they are no longer set apart for holy use. Their mention in Revelation 18:13 reflects how the sacred provisions of the covenant were squandered in pursuit of luxury and power.

Fine Flour, Wheat, Beasts, and Sheep

Once the lifeblood of Temple offerings, these sacrificial elements (Leviticus 2:1–16; 24:5–9) become nothing more than trade goods in the harlot's empire—a chilling picture of worship reduced to economics, and sacrifice to self-interest.

Horses, Chariots, Slaves, and Souls of Men

Here the portrait darkens further. These final items, while not part of the Temple ritual, expose the dehumanization at the heart of apostate Jerusalem's corruption. Oppression has replaced justice. Exploitation has supplanted mercy. The city meant to be a light to the nations has become a trafficker of souls.

The Adornment of the Harlot: From Sacred to Profane

John's description of the harlot's garments and treasures is not incidental. He is pointing us back to the Temple, to the holy vestments, the golden vessels, and the precious stones that once reflected the beauty of God's presence. But now, in the hands of the harlot, these same elements signal decay. What was sacred has been made vulgar. What was pure has been sold. The very glory entrusted to Jerusalem has been turned into her downfall.

This is the tragedy of apostasy: that which was meant to reveal God to the world becomes a stumbling block. Jerusalem, once the faithful bride, is now exposed as the unfaithful woman, seducing rather than sanctifying, consuming rather than consecrating.

The evidence is overwhelming. The mirrors between the treasures of Babylon and the treasures of the Temple are too precise to ignore. These were not merely economic goods. They were once holy things. And in the hands of the harlot, they become emblems of betrayal, markers of a city that exchanged her divine calling for fleeting pleasures and corrupt power.

Thus, the fall of Babylon is not just the collapse of a corrupt system; it is the judgment of a city that once knew God and turned away. It is the closing chapter of a covenant violated, a bride forsaken, and a kingdom squandered.

Yet even in this sobering revelation, there remains a call, a warning for us all to examine our hearts and our worship. Are we stewarding the treasures of God for His glory? Or have we, too, allowed the sacred to become common, the holy to become profane?

The Silencing of Joy and Industry: Jeremiah's Prophecy and Mystery Babylon

One of the most chilling images woven through the tapestry of Revelation is not the clash of armies or the fall of empires, but the profound and absolute silencing of life. When Mystery Babylon collapses, her downfall is marked not merely by destruction, but by the extinguishing of joy itself—a city once bustling with music, celebration, and labor reduced to a mournful silence.

This echoes the ancient words of Jeremiah, who prophesied judgment upon Jerusalem with haunting finality:

"Moreover I will take from them the voice of mirth, and the voice of gladness, the voice of the bridegroom, and the voice of the bride, the sound of the millstones, and the light of the candle." (Jeremiah 25:10)

These are not merely poetic expressions. They signify the collapse of everyday life—of weddings and work, of laughter and labor. The sounds that once filled the streets of the holy city would be heard no more. The reason? Idolatry. Injustice. Betrayal of covenant.

Centuries later, in Revelation 18:22–23, the same dirge is sung over Babylon:

And the voice of harpers, and musicians, and of pipers, and trumpeters, shall be heard no more at all in thee; and no craftsman, of whatsoever craft he be, shall be found any more in thee; and the sound of a millstone shall be heard no more at all in thee;

And the light of a candle shall shine no more at all in thee; and the voice of the bridegroom and of the bride shall be heard no more at all in thee: for thy merchants were the great men of the earth; for by thy sorceries were all nations deceived.

The parallels are deliberate. Revelation is invoking Jeremiah's lament, lifting the imagery of Jerusalem's fall and placing it over Babylon—a symbolic Jerusalem now fully given over to spiritual harlotry. What God once withdrew from His covenant city due to her unfaithfulness, He now removes from Babylon in the fullness of judgment. The harlot, clothed in stolen glory, ends in silence and darkness.

The ceasing of music and the dimming of lamps symbolize not just the end of a city, but the end of purpose, the end of divine presence, the end of covenant blessing. The only safeguard against such silence is faithfulness—a return to the Lamb and the light that no darkness can overcome.

Mourning and the Pilots: The Lamentation over Tyre and Babylon

As Revelation unveils the fall of Babylon, we hear the echo of yet another ancient lament. The mourning of the merchants, shipmasters, and mariners is not a new song, but one first sung over Tyre, the great trading city of Ezekiel's prophecy.

In Ezekiel 27:28–32, the scene unfolds with raw, ritual grief:

"The suburbs shall shake at the sound of the cry of thy pilots.

And all that handle the oar, the mariners, and all the pilots of the sea, shall come down from their ships, they shall stand upon the land; And shall cause their voice to be heard against thee, and shall cry bitterly,

and shall cast up dust upon their heads, they shall wallow themselves in the ashes: And they shall make themselves utterly bald for thee, and gird them with sackcloth, and they shall weep for thee with bitterness of heart and bitter wailing.

And in their wailing they shall take up a lamentation for thee, and lament over thee, saying, What city is like Tyrus, like the destroyed in the midst of the sea?"

These were the ones who prospered from Tyre's wealth. They handled her cargo, sailed her ships, and built their fortunes on her success. And when Tyre fell, they stood ashore, mourning not only the city, but the loss of their own security, comfort, and gain.

The same scene is replayed in Revelation 18:17–19:

"For in one hour so great riches is come to nought. And every shipmaster, and all the company in ships, and sailors, and as many as trade by sea, stood afar off, And cried when they saw the smoke of her burning, saying, What city is like unto this great city! And they cast dust on their heads, and cried, weeping, and wailing, saying, Alas, alas that great city, wherein were made rich all that had ships in the sea by reason of her costliness! for in one hour is she made desolate."

Their sorrow is not for Babylon's soul, but for their own loss. Commerce has been interrupted. Luxury has been stripped away. The empire of excess has collapsed in an hour. The hour of the cross!

Through these parallel laments, Scripture paints a sobering picture: the kingdoms of this world are fragile. The markets rise and fall. Empires built on exploitation, greed, and idolatry will not stand. And when they fall, those who placed their hope in them are left with nothing but ashes and empty hands.

But for the faithful, these scenes are not given to provoke despair—they are reminders of the transience of earthly wealth and the certainty of divine justice. Tyre fell. Babylon fell. Every system that exalts itself against the knowledge of God will fall. Yet, in the midst of every collapse, the Kingdom of God endures.

And so we are called to place our trust not in the fleeting riches of Babylon, but in the unshakable city whose architect and builder is God. We are invited to forsake the fleeting ships of commerce and cast our lot with the Lamb, whose reign has no end.

For while the merchants mourn, the Bride prepares. While Babylon burns, the New Jerusalem descends. And as the laments rise from the earth, the song of the redeemed rises higher still.

Conclusion: From the Fall of Babylon to the Rise of the Bride

As we bring our exploration of Mystery Babylon to its end, we are reminded that the symbols of Scripture are never mere ornament.

They are windows into eternal truths, beckoning us to look deeper—to see beyond the surface, to discern the patterns of faithfulness and failure that echo across time.

In the rise and fall of Babylon, in the judgment of apostate Jerusalem, and in the descent of the New Jerusalem, we witness not only the outworking of Old Testament prophecy but the unfolding story of redemption and restoration.

For Babylon's fall is not the end of the narrative. Judgment, though fierce and just, clears the ground for something greater—the revealing of God's Kingdom, a city not built by human hands, but prepared as a Bride adorned for her Husband. And as we walk through these prophetic visions, we find ourselves woven into this story. We, the Body of Christ, are called to embody the very hope that triumphs over the ashes of rebellion.

The prophet Isaiah's words still resound through the ages:

"For Zion's sake will I not hold my peace, and for Jerusalem's sake I will not rest, until the righteousness thereof go forth as brightness, and the salvation thereof as a lamp that burneth." (Isaiah 62:1)

Here lies the heartbeat of Revelation's mystery. Mystery Babylon is a caution—a solemn reminder of the dangers of spiritual compromise, the seduction of idolatry, and the consequences of turning away from the living God. Her fall warns every generation: Beware the subtle drift from covenant fidelity. Beware the temptation to trade holiness for power, and worship for wealth.

And yet, amid the shadows of judgment, grace still shines. As Jerusalem was offered renewal despite her unfaithfulness, so too is every heart invited back into the embrace of mercy. The hand of God remains outstretched. The voice of the Spirit still calls: "Come out of her, My people." Abandon the comforts of compromise. Return to the Lamb.

In our modern age—an era no less susceptible to the allure of Babylon's promises—we must guard our hearts with vigilance. Let us reject the subtle lies of spiritual adultery, the lure of cultural idolatry, and the complacency of a faith grown cold. Let us be found faithful. Let us be found watching.

And as the kingdoms of this world rise and fall, as empires come and go, may we remember that only one Kingdom endures. Only one Name prevails. And in the Lamb, we discover our unshakable hope, our unfailing refuge, and our eternal home.

So, with courage and conviction, let us press on. The same God who brought down Babylon, who judged the apostate Jerusalem, the unfaithful city, and who descended the New Jerusalem, remains sovereign over history. He is the same yesterday, today, and forever. And His promises are sure.

Where have we traded purity for power? Where have we flaunted beauty that was never ours to wear? Babylon may wear the crown for a moment—but her fall was certain.

And you—you are invited to rise. To be the Bride. To be radiant and ready.

May we carry these truths as we journey forward—eyes fixed on the Lamb, hearts anchored in grace, and lives shaped by the unwavering certainty that the Kingdom of God has come, and its gates are open wide to all who will enter in faith and faithfulness.

Key Takeaways:

Mystery Babylon, the Great Harlot, symbolically represents apostate Jerusalem—the city that betrayed its covenant with God by rejecting the Messiah and embracing idolatry.

Her adornment and "merchandise" are deliberate parallels to the sacred items of the Jerusalem Temple, now profaned by spiritual unfaithfulness and self-exaltation.

Jerusalem's judgment and silence, echoing Old Testament prophecies against unfaithful cities like Tyre, signify the end of the Old Covenant order and a warning against spiritual compromise in any age.

Chapter 4

THE SCARLET BEAST: SIN AND THE LAW

The Scarlet Beast: Symbol of Sin in Revelation

In the majestic narrative of Revelation 17 and 18, the scarlet beast emerges as a profound symbol of sin's pervasive nature and its spiritual consequences.

To fully comprehend this symbolism, we embark on a journey through these passages, decoding the intricate elements of the scarlet beast.

Our exploration will weave together the moral framework of the Ten Commandments, the spiritual significance of the Seven Feast Days of Israel, and the apostle Paul's profound teachings in Romans regarding the law and sin.

Additionally, insights from Proverbs 6 on the seven abominations hated by the Lord will deepen our understanding of sin's insidious influence.

Revelation 17 presents a striking vision: a scarlet beast bearing the Great Harlot, a potent symbol of idolatry, immorality, and spiritual corruption—first-century apostate Jerusalem.

The beast, scarlet in color, with seven heads and ten horns, invites us to delve into its symbolic significance.

The scarlet hue, often associated with sin and iniquity, resonates with Isaiah 1:18: "Come now, and let us reason together, saith the Lord: though your sins be as scarlet, they shall be as white as snow."

As we established in the previous chapter, the Harlot who rides this beast is adorned with corrupted holy things from the Temple. It follows logically that the Beast she rides upon represents a corruption of the holy systems God gave to Israel. Therefore, to understand its symbolic parts—the seven heads and ten horns—we should look to God's most sacred structural appointments: His divine laws and His sacred festivals.

The seven heads and ten horns of the scarlet beast gain clarity when linked to the moral compass of the Ten Commandments and the spiritual tapestry of the Seven Feast Days of Israel. The Commandments, etched in stone by God's own hand, establish divine standards of righteous living. The ten horns, however, suggest a distortion and misuse of these divine laws, leading to sinful behavior—much like the way the Pharisees and religious leaders of Jesus' time twisted the law to serve their own ends. Similarly, the seven heads symbolize the Seven Feast Days of Israel (Leviticus 23), which, when misinterpreted or observed superficially, become conduits for spiritual corruption.

In Proverbs 6:16–19, the seven abominations the Lord hates provide a framework for understanding this corruption: "These six things doth the Lord hate: yea, seven are an abomination unto him: A proud look, a lying tongue, and hands that shed innocent blood, An heart that deviseth wicked imaginations, feet that be swift in running to mischief, A false witness that speaketh lies, and he that soweth discord among brethren." These abominations reflect the attributes of the scarlet beast and the Whore of Babylon—pride, deceit, violence, and division, all leading to spiritual decay.

The Law and the Feasts: Shadows Consumed by the Beast

The Scarlet Beast is not merely symbolic of corrupt institutions or false religion—it is the personification of sin itself. Not just sin in its vulgar forms, but sin cloaked in robes of righteousness, parading as godliness. It is the deceptive, inward corruption that thrives within religious systems when form replaces faith and ritual overshadows relationship. This beast, full of names of blasphemy, represents the carnal mind exalting itself through works, self-righteousness, and rebellion against the Spirit.

Consider how this beast system made use of what was once sacred. It took the very foundation of God's covenant with Israel—the Ten Commandments—and transformed them from a mirror of sin into a measuring stick of pride. The Law, which was holy and just and good, became a weapon of condemnation when wielded apart from the Spirit. As Paul wrote, "For the letter killeth, but the spirit giveth life" (2 Corinthians 3:6). The beast of sin takes what is good and twists it into a means of boasting, control, and guilt. It points to the commandments but not to Christ, in whom alone the righteousness of the law is fulfilled (Romans 8:3–4).

In the same way, the Seven Feast Days of the Lord—which prophetically pointed to Christ's redemptive work—were devoured by this beastly system and reduced to empty rituals. Passover spoke of the Lamb slain, Unleavened Bread of a sinless life, Firstfruits of the resurrection, Pentecost of the Spirit's outpouring, and Trumpets, Atonement, and Tabernacles of the judgment, covering, and indwelling presence of God. These were never ends in themselves—they were shadows of Christ (Colossians 2:16–17). But the beast of sin, always resisting the Spirit, clung to the shadow and rejected the substance.

This is the true nature of the Scarlet Beast: sin concealed beneath ceremonial piety. It is the spirit of religion that honors God with its lips but whose heart is far from Him. It parades commandments and feast days, not to glorify Christ but to exalt the self. It is not a beast of horns and crowns but of pride, self-justification, and spiritual blindness. This is the beast that John saw—a grotesque image of sin disguised as righteousness, deceiving many who worship the outward form but never surrender to inward transformation.

Sin and the Law

Paul's letter to the Romans offers a nuanced understanding of the interplay between the law and sin. In Romans 7:8–9, he articulates the internal struggle, acknowledging the holiness of the law yet revealing humanity's propensity to transgress: "But sin, taking occasion by the commandment, wrought in me all manner of concupiscence. For without the law, sin was dead."

This intricate dance between sin and the law echoes in Revelation's narrative. The Whore of Babylon, riding upon the scarlet beast, becomes a metaphor for the manipulation and misuse of religious and moral principles under the law. This also reflects the subjugation of sin to apostate Jerusalem, which clung to the letter of the law while neglecting its spirit. Ultimately, the scarlet beast, embodying sin, devours the Whore, symbolizing the inevitable consequences of sin when it exploits the law.

The Beast's Judgment on the Harlot

As we delve deeper into the symbolism of Revelation 17 and 18, we must consider the relationship between the law, sin, and the scarlet beast. This connection is vividly portrayed in Revelation 17:12–13, where the horns, representing the law, lend their power to the beast, symbolizing sin.

"And the ten horns which thou sawest are ten kings, which have received no kingdom as yet; but receive power as kings one hour with the beast. These have one mind, and shall give their power and strength unto the beast." This passage illustrates how the horns, symbolizing the authority and power of the law, bolster the beast. While the law, in its pure form, is intended to guide and direct, when manipulated by sin, it becomes a tool for destruction.

Paul's letter to the Romans sheds further light on this dynamic.

Romans 7:8–9 explains, "But sin, taking occasion by the commandment, wrought in me all manner of concupiscence.

For without the law, sin was dead.

For I was alive without the law once: but when the commandment came, sin revived, and I died." Paul illuminates how the law, though holy, exposes, and even amplifies sin's power.

The law's function is to reveal sin, but in a spiritually fallen apostate Jerusalem, it empowers sin as humanity's inherent rebellious nature exploits the law's commandments.

The Beast, Horns, and the Harlot

Revelation 17:16 continues, "And the ten horns which thou sawest upon the beast, these shall hate the whore, and shall make her desolate and naked, and shall eat her flesh, and burn her with fire." This graphic imagery symbolizes the ultimate judgment and destruction of apostate Jerusalem.

The city, unable to uphold the law written on stone, succumbs to the very sin the law sought to restrain.

External adherence to the law proves insufficient, highlighting the need for internal transformation—a theme echoed throughout Scripture.

Jeremiah 31:33 foretells this necessary shift: "But this shall be the covenant that I will make with the house of Israel; After those days, saith the Lord, I will put my law in their inward parts, and write it in their hearts; and will be their God, and they shall be my people. This new covenant emphasizes a transformation that goes beyond external adherence to the law, requiring the law to be internalized and written on the hearts of the people.

The Law on Stone vs. the Law on Hearts: Fulfilled Promise

The law, while righteous and holy, was never sufficient to keep sin in check when written only on stone tablets.

Jerusalem's history is a testament to this truth.

Despite having the law, the city fell into repeated cycles of sin and rebellion.

Romans 8:3–4 highlights this inadequacy: "For what the law could not do, in that it was weak through the flesh, God sending his own Son in the likeness of sinful flesh, and for sin, condemned sin in the flesh: That the righteousness of the law might be fulfilled in us, who walk not after the flesh, but after the Spirit."

This passage underscores the necessity of the law being fulfilled through Christ and internalized within believers. The law alone, external, and imposed, could not achieve true righteousness. It had to be complemented by the transformative power of the Spirit, enabling believers to embody the law's principles genuinely.

One Hour: Judgment and Redemption

Revelation 17:12 mentions the horns receiving power as kings "one hour with the beast." This reference to "one hour" is significant when viewed in the context of Jesus' crucifixion.

Jesus often spoke of His "hour" as the moment of His suffering and crucifixion.

In John 12:23 Jesus says, "The hour has come for the Son of Man to be glorified." This hour is further illuminated in John 19:14, which describes the events leading up to His crucifixion: "Now it was the day of Preparation of the Passover; it was about the sixth hour.

He said to the Jews, 'Behold your King!'

This critical "hour" represents not just a moment in time but the culmination of Jesus' mission to redeem humanity through His sacrifice.

Revelation 18:10 adds another layer of significance to this concept, stating, "Standing afar off for the fear of her torment, saying, Alas, alas, that great city Babylon, that mighty city! For in one hour is thy judgment come." This verse underscores the sudden and swift nature of Babylon's judgment, paralleling the decisive and transformative "hour" of Jesus' crucifixion.

This 'one hour' links two worlds: the hour of Christ's obedience unto death, and the hour of judgment upon the system that crucified Him.

In one, grace triumphed.

In the other, judgment fell.

Revelation 18:17 also refers to a significant hour: "For in one hour so great riches is come to nought." This hour of great loss corresponds to the hour of the cross, where Jesus' sacrifice upended the powers of sin and death. Just as the horns lend their power to the beast for "one hour," leading to the beast devouring the Whore. Jesus' hour at the cross symbolizes the ultimate defeat of sin and the old covenant, ushering in a new era of grace where the law is written on believers' hearts.

Final Defeat of Sin and Satan: The Final Triumph

The final triumph over sin is vividly depicted in Revelation 20:10: "And the devil that deceived them was cast into the lake of fire and brimstone, where the beast and the false prophet are, and shall be tormented day and night for ever and ever." This eternal torment signifies the ultimate victory of the Christian over sin, made possible through the redemptive work of Jesus Christ.

The defeat of Satan, the beast, and the false prophet highlights the culmination of the spiritual battle, where the forces of evil are permanently vanquished.

This torment and defeat are tied to the victory that Christians have over sin through Jesus' sacrifice.

Romans 2:12 underscores this, stating, "For as many as have sinned without law shall also perish without law: and as many as have sinned in the law shall be judged by the law." The Jews, having the law, perished by the law, while the Gentiles, without the law, perished without it.

This highlights the insufficiency of the law alone and the necessity of the internal transformation brought by Christ.

The Law Amplifies Sin

Paul delves deeper into the nature of sin and its relationship with the law in Romans 7:13: "Was then that which is good made death unto me? God forbid. But sin, that it might appear sin, working death in me by that which is good; that sin by the commandment might become exceeding sinful." This passage reveals the paradox of the law: while it is good, it inadvertently magnifies sin by providing a standard that our sinful nature inevitably rebels against.

This echoes the narrative of the scarlet beast. The scarlet tone, signifying sin, intensifies when intertwined with the law. The ten horns, symbolizing the distortion and misuse of God's moral laws, highlight how sin, amplified by the law, becomes exceedingly sinful, mirroring the destructive consequences depicted in Revelation.

Seven Heads and the Eighth Beast: The Symbolism

The imagery of the scarlet beast with its seven heads presents a compelling depiction of sin's multifaceted nature.

These seven heads symbolize the culmination of sin's manifestations throughout history, encompassing various forms of rebellion and disobedience against God.

In Revelation 17:9–10, we encounter an intriguing interpretation of these heads as seven mountains, representing both kingdoms and kings.

This imagery suggests a symbolic representation of the pervasive influence of sin across different epochs and realms of human existence.

However, amidst the symbolism of the seven heads, an enigmatic figure emerges—the scarlet beast itself, described as the eighth but also as one of the seven (Revelation 17:11). This paradoxical portrayal signifies the culmination and embodiment of sin's ultimate rebellion against God. The beast, "having been, is not, and yet is," denotes sin's enduring presence and persistence despite temporal fluctuations and the redemptive work of Christ.

Sin Under Law vs. Grace Under Faith: The New Covenant

The concept of sin under the law finds resonance in the scarlet beast's portrayal as one of the seven heads. Under the Mosaic Law, sin was codified and delineated, providing a clear moral framework for righteous living. However, this legalistic approach to sin merely exposed humanity's inherent rebellious nature, as articulated by Paul in Romans 7:7–8. The scarlet hue of the beast symbolizes the sinfulness inherent in transgressions under the law, stained crimson with disobedience.

With the advent of Christ and the inauguration of the New Covenant, the sacrificial shedding of His blood offered atonement for sin, ushering in an era of grace and redemption.

Yet despite the efficacy of Christ's atonement, sin remains a pervasive reality in the human experience.

The scarlet beast as the eighth signifies sin's persistence even in the face of divine grace and forgiveness.

While believers are no longer under the condemnation of the law (Romans 8:1), the presence of sin still necessitates continual reliance on the cleansing power of Christ's blood (1 John 1:7).

The designation of the scarlet beast having seven heads, yet also as the eighth, underscores the timeless reality of sin's existence.

Sin, having been present since the Fall, continues to exert its influence in the world, manifesting in various forms of moral, spiritual, and societal decay.

The scarlet beast's paradoxical nature reflects sin's ability to adapt and persist throughout history, remaining a formidable adversary in the ongoing spiritual battle.

This scarlet beast, representing sin, can be temporarily controlled by spiritual apostate Jerusalem, but eventually, the battle is lost.

Sin became exceedingly sinful when the law, the ten horns, lends its power to the beast.

Seven Appearances of Satan: A Short Space

Within the book of Revelation, we encounter a cryptic passage in Revelation 17:10 concerning seven kings: "And there are seven kings: five are fallen, and one is, and the other is not yet come; and when he cometh, he must continue a short space." When interpreted symbolically within the context of Revelation itself, these kings represent the various appearances or manifestations of Satan or his persona within the narrative. Let's explore these appearances and their spiritual significance:

The five fallen kings symbolize the previous appearances or encounters with Satan within the narrative of Revelation.

These could include instances such as the dragon's attempt to devour the child in Revelation 12, the beast rising from the sea in Revelation 13, the dragon giving power to the beast in Revelation.

13:2, the dragon persecuting the woman in Revelation 12:13, and the dragon making war with the remnant of the woman's seed in Revelation 12:17.

Each of these encounters represents a distinct episode where Satan or his influence is prominently featured.

The king that "is" represents the present reality of Satan's activity within the narrative. This could signify ongoing events such as the beast's persecution of the saints in Revelation 13 or the deception of the nations by the false prophet in Revelation 19:20. In this current epoch of the narrative, Satan continues his schemes to deceive and corrupt humanity, seeking to oppose God's kingdom and hinder His purposes.

The Other Is Not Yet Come and the Short Space: This future king symbolizes a forthcoming appearance or manifestation of Satan's influence within the narrative. The reference to "a short space" in Revelation 17:10 holds significant meaning within the narrative of Revelation itself. This aligns with events such as Satan being loosed from the bottomless pit in Revelation 20:7–8, where "he must be loosed a little season."

Conclusion: Grace Overcomes the Beast

In conclusion, the symbolism of the scarlet beast with its seven heads and ten horns offers profound insights into the nature of sin and its enduring presence in human experience.

While sin was exposed under the law and mitigated through the blood of Christ, its persistent existence underscores the ongoing need for vigilance, repentance, and reliance on God's grace.

As believers navigate the complexities of a fallen world, may they find solace in the redemptive power of Christ, who overcame sin and death, offering hope and restoration to all who believe.

The beast was sin. The ten horns were the law. The seven heads represent the feast days. The Whore was the city that once clung to the law—until that law empowered the sin that consumed her.

The beast has no power over those who walk by grace. For what was once scarlet has been washed white—and now shines with the brilliance of the Lamb.

Key Takeaways:

The Scarlet Beast is a profound symbol of sin's pervasive nature and the legalistic system of the Old Covenant that empowered it, rather than a future world dictator.

Its seven heads and ten horns represent the distortion and misuse of God's moral laws and spiritual principles under the Old Covenant, leading to spiritual decay.

The Beast devouring the Harlot symbolizes the inevitable consequences of sin when it exploits the law, highlighting the insufficiency of external adherence and the necessity of internal transformation through Christ.

Chapter 5

VICTORY OF CHRIST: THIS IS MY BELOVED SON

The Cosmic Battle Unveiled: A Spiritual War

The Book of Revelation presents a cosmic narrative that transcends time, place, and tradition—a sweeping vision that peels back the veil between the seen and unseen realms. Within this majestic vision emerges one of Revelation's most vivid and formidable symbols: the Dragon.

This Dragon, cloaked in fiery red and crowned with a false sense of dominion, stands as the embodiment of spiritual rebellion.

He is not merely a creature of chaos, but the great adversary who has, since the beginning, opposed the purposes of God.

His war is waged not only in the heavenly realms but also through deception and persecution against God's covenant people on earth.

He is the unseen hand behind the systems of oppression, false religion, and fear that have plagued the people of God throughout the ages.

Yet as terrifying as this figure may seem, it is crucial to understand that the Dragon is not the focal point of the Revelation.

His wrath, though real, is reactionary.

His opposition, though intense, is rooted in desperation.

His power is not sovereign—it is permitted and ultimately overridden by divine purpose.

The central message of Revelation, and indeed of this chapter, is not the magnitude of evil, but the majesty of Christ.

The spotlight does not linger on the roar of the Dragon, but on the triumph of the Lamb.

Throughout this chapter, we will examine the Dragon's role within the broader spiritual conflict and trace the contours of his symbolic presence as detailed in Revelation 12.

We will uncover how his opposition plays into a larger redemptive arc—an arc that reveals, not defeat for the faithful, but victory through the all-sufficient sacrifice of the Lamb.

The narrative reveals that the Dragon's fall is not a deferred promise to fear, but a spiritual unveiling already secured through the death, resurrection, and exaltation of Christ.

We will also consider how this vision fits within the larger message already established in earlier chapters: that the Kingdom of God is present and the symbols of Revelation unfold not as literal disasters, but as spiritual truths with real implications for the Church. The story of the Dragon is not a detour from that vision—it is a confirmation of it. It affirms that even in the presence of opposition, the reign of Christ is secure and unshaken.

This chapter invites us to see beyond the surface—to discern the spiritual realities concealed within prophetic symbols.

As we explore the heavenly conflict and the Dragon's furious resistance, we do so with the confidence that the battle has already been won, the accuser has already been cast down, and the Church stands not in peril, but in promise.

The Woman and the Child: A Vision of Redemptive Triumph

Immediately after the Dragon's introduction, Revelation 12 unveils a second profound vision that reveals the unfolding of God's redemptive plan through the people of the covenant:

"And there appeared a great wonder in heaven; a woman clothed with the sun, and the moon under her feet, and upon her head a crown of twelve stars:

And she being with child cried, travailing in birth, and pained to be delivered." (Revelation 12:1–2)

This woman represents Israel, not as a physical nation, but as the faithful covenant community chosen by God to bring forth the Messiah. She is clothed with the sun—radiant in God's righteousness and favor. The moon under her feet symbolizes the reflected glory of the old covenant system, now being fulfilled. Her crown of twelve stars points unmistakably to the twelve tribes of Israel—establishing her identity as the bearer of divine promise.

That promise begins its ultimate fulfillment in this heavenly vision. The woman groans in labor—symbolizing the spiritual and historical travail of Israel as she anticipates the coming of the Messiah. The birth pangs encompass the entire arc of redemptive history—from the patriarchs and prophets to the exiles, persecutions, and cries for deliverance that rose from the faithful remnant.

Then, the child is born.

"And she brought forth a man child, who was to rule all nations with a rod of iron:

and her child was caught up unto God, and to his throne." (Revelation 12:5)

The child is unmistakably Jesus Christ, the long-awaited King and Redeemer. The imagery of ruling "with a rod of iron" directly fulfills the messianic prophecy in Psalm 2:7–9, where the Father says to the Son:

"Thou art my Son; this day have I begotten thee.

Ask of me, and I shall give thee the heathen for thine inheritance,

and the uttermost parts of the earth for thy possession.

Thou shalt break them with a rod of iron;

thou shalt dash them in pieces like a potter's vessel."

This is not a prophecy of future military conquest, but of present spiritual rule—a dominion established by truth and Spirit over sin and death. The child being "caught up unto God, and to his throne" is a symbolic portrayal of Jesus' enthronement at baptism, as we will see. The emphasis is not on the threat posed by the Dragon, but on the protection, exaltation, and heavenly authority of Christ.

The vision also finds typological expression in the earthly narrative of Christ's birth.

Just as the Dragon stands ready to devour the child in Revelation, so too did Herod seek to destroy the Christ child at the moment of His arrival.

Herod, acting under satanic influence, issued a decree to kill all male children under the age of two in Bethlehem (Matthew 2:16), hoping to extinguish the Light before it could shine.

But just as God preserved the child in Revelation 12, so too did He protect Jesus by leading Joseph and Mary to flee to Egypt.

Herod, like the Dragon, failed.

The typology is unmistakable—earthly events mirror spiritual truths.

Moreover, the woman's flight into the wilderness (Revelation 12:6) also reflects Israel's historic pattern of divine preservation in times of crisis— from the exodus out of Egypt to the exile and return. It is the unified covenant people of God, the faithful Israel through whom the Messiah comes and to whom the promises are fulfilled.

Thus, the vision in Revelation 12 is not isolated. It is a spiritual composite of prophetic fulfillment, messianic triumph, and covenant continuity. It demonstrates that the redemptive arc has reached its pinnacle in Christ and that the Dragon's schemes—whether through Herod, legalism, or persecution—cannot prevail against the purposes of God.

The War in Heaven: Defeat on a Spiritual Plane

Revelation 12:7–9 unveils a majestic and decisive conflict:

"And there was war in heaven: Michael and his angels fought against the dragon; and the dragon fought and his angels,

and prevailed not; neither was their place found any more in heaven. And the great dragon was cast out, that old serpent,

called the Devil, and Satan, which deceiveth the whole world: he was cast out into the earth, and his angels were cast out with him."

This cosmic battle is not merely symbolic (it reflects a transformative spiritual reality. The language of war may evoke images of swords and bloodshed, but the true nature of this conflict is jurisdictional and covenantal. This is not a battle fought with physical weapons, but with authority, testimony, and triumph. The outcome is a spiritual transition: the removal of Satan)—the accuser—from his position in the heavenly courts.

This "casting out" is not an event to come in the distant future—it was already fulfilled during the ministry of Jesus. In Luke 10:17–18 after the seventy disciples return from their mission with joy, declaring that "even the devils are subject unto us through thy name," Jesus responds:

"I beheld Satan as lightning fall from heaven."

Here, Jesus is not prophesying a future fall—He is announcing a present manifested truth. The kingdom of God was advancing, and the reign of the accuser was collapsing.

The Accuser Cast Down: Christ's Victory and Our Testimony

Every healing, every deliverance, every declaration of the gospel was a blow to Satan's dominion. Christ had come not only to atone for sin but to disarm the accuser, fulfilling the prophetic hope of Genesis 3:15, where the seed of the woman would crush the serpent's head.

This spiritual victory finds its formal and symbolic expression in Revelation 12. The war is waged in heaven, but the battlefield is legal authority. Satan is defeated, not by power alone, but by truth. Revelation 12:10–11 affirms this:

"Now is come salvation, and strength, and the kingdom of our God, and the power of his Christ:

for the accuser of our brethren is cast down, which accused them before our God day and night.

And they overcame him by the blood of the Lamb, and by the word of their testimony…"

This victory belongs to Christ and to His people—not because of their performance, but because of their position in Christ. The accuser's access is cut off; his case is dismissed. The courtroom of heaven no longer entertains his charges. The righteousness of Christ has forever silenced the voice of condemnation against those who are in Him.

In this heavenly legal drama, Michael emerges as a central figure. In Daniel 10:13, 21, and Daniel 12:1, Michael is described as the great prince who stands for the children of God's people. His role is consistently that of a protector—one who wars against the forces that oppose God's covenant purposes. In Revelation 12, Michael leads the angelic host in casting the Dragon out, fulfilling his role as the defender of the faithful.

Some have suggested that Michael may be a pre-incarnate manifestation of Christ, similar to the "Angel of the Lord" who appears throughout the Old Testament.

While this interpretation remains debated, what cannot be denied is that Michael's actions mirror the mission of Christ: confronting the enemy, defending God's people, and executing divine judgment.

Whether Michael is a distinct angelic being or a title pointing to the preexistent Christ, the outcome remains the same—the enemy is defeated, and the heavens are purified.

This war in heaven is a spiritual and judicial battle, and it finds an earthly echo in the temptations of Christ in the wilderness. Before beginning His public ministry, Jesus confronted Satan directly. In Matthew 4:1–11, we see the Dragon's strategy: question Christ's identity, challenge His trust in the Father, and offer Him the kingdoms of the world apart from the cross. Yet Jesus overcame every temptation with Scripture:

"It is written, Man shall not live by bread alone, but by every word that proceedeth out of the mouth of God." (Matthew 4:4)

"It is written again, Thou shalt not tempt the Lord thy God." (Matthew 4:7)

"Get thee hence, Satan: for it is written, Thou shalt worship the Lord thy God, and him only shalt thou serve." (Matthew 4:10)

At the end of this confrontation:

"Then the devil leaveth him, and, behold, angels came and ministered unto him." (Matthew 4:11)

This event is more than a personal victory—it is the earthly manifestation of the heavenly war. Christ resisted the Dragon's temptations and stood as the second Adam, victorious where the first had fallen. This moment, paired with the cross and the ascension, seals the Dragon's fate. As Jesus later declared:

"Now is the judgment of this world: now shall the prince of this world be cast out." (John 12:31)

The Baptism and Temptation of Christ: The Spiritual Battle Begins

The war in heaven depicted in Revelation 12 finds one of its most striking earthly reflections in the baptism and temptation of Jesus Christ. This is not a disconnected narrative—it is the very initiation of the redemptive war that would culminate in the cross, resurrection, and exaltation of the Son.

The Gospels reveal this pivotal moment:

"And Jesus, when he was baptized, went up straightway out of the water: and, lo, the heavens were opened unto him, and he saw the Spirit of God descending like a dove, and lighting upon him: And lo a voice from heaven, saying, This is my beloved Son, in whom I am well pleased." (Matthew 3:16-17)

Here, the heavens open and the Spirit descends—mirroring the child being "caught up unto God and to His throne." (Revelation 12:5) This is more than a commissioning; it is a public declaration of Sonship, authority, and divine approval. The Father's voice reverberates with covenantal power: "This is my beloved Son." It is the beginning of the war.

Immediately, the Spirit leads Jesus into the wilderness:

"Then was Jesus led up of the Spirit into the wilderness to be tempted of the devil." (Matthew 4:1)

There, after forty days of fasting—forty being a number often associated with testing and transition—He faces the Dragon directly. The temptations are not random; they strike at the heart of Christ's identity and mission:

"If thou be the Son of God…" (Matthew 4:3)

"Command that these stones be made bread." (Matthew 4:3)

"Cast thyself down…" (Matthew 4:6)

"All these [kingdoms] will I give thee…" (Matthew 4:9)

Each temptation parallels the satanic desire to usurp, accuse, and destroy. Yet Jesus overcomes not through spectacle, but by the Word.

This is the spiritual battle. It is here that the Dragon is cast down—not with sword and shield, but through truth, obedience, and unwavering identity in the Father's will.

Just as Revelation 12 speaks of the accuser being overcome "by the blood of the Lamb, and by the word of their testimony" (Revelation 12:11), Jesus overcomes by the Word and His obedience. He is the true and faithful Israel, the greater Adam, and the victorious Son.

His baptism and temptation are not simply prologue—they are the opening salvo of the great spiritual war that Revelation reveals. The Child is caught up; the Dragon is enraged; the saints overcome through Him.

The Dragon's Rage: A Time of Persecution

Revelation 12:12 offers a sobering proclamation:

"Woe to the inhabiters of the earth and of the sea! for the devil is come down unto you, having great wrath, because he knoweth that he hath but a short time."

Though defeated in heaven, the Dragon turns his fury toward the earth, spiritually. No longer able to accuse from above, he now deceives, persecutes, and seeks to destroy from below. This is not evidence of his power, but of his desperation. The Cross has broken his claim; the Resurrection has stripped his authority.

The Earth Helps the Woman: God's Sovereign Protection

Revelation 12:16 paints a beautiful picture of divine intervention:

"And the earth helped the woman, and the earth opened her mouth, and swallowed up the flood which the dragon cast out of his mouth."

The flood represents a torrent of deception, persecution, or spiritual attack unleashed against the covenant community. But creation itself, under the command of the Creator, comes to the aid of the woman. This is no accident—this is sovereignty in action.

The imagery echoes back to the Exodus, when the Red Sea swallowed Pharaoh's armies, protecting God's people from annihilation. It reminds us that the Church's preservation is not merely spiritual but also historical and providential.

Wilderness Typology: A Pattern of Preservation

The woman's flight into the wilderness also echoes a profound biblical pattern of divine preservation. Just as God led Israel out of Egypt and sustained her with manna and water in the wilderness, so too does He protect His covenant people in times of trial. Elijah, too, was nourished by ravens in a barren land. Christ Himself was led by the Spirit into the wilderness, where He overcame temptation.

In each case, the wilderness is not a place of abandonment, but of preparation and divine encounter. Revelation 12 continues this thread— God's people are spiritually sustained even when outwardly pressed. The wilderness becomes a sanctuary, a proving ground, and a space of provision ordained by God.

The Dragon's Final Assault: War on the Remnant

Revelation 12:17 concludes:

"And the dragon was wroth with the woman, and went to make war with the remnant of her seed, which keep the commandments of God, and have the testimony of Jesus Christ."

—The harlot is judged. The Bride is unveiled.

The Dragon, defeated, and enraged, now targets the remnant—the faithful who hold fast to the testimony of Jesus. These are not passive victims; they are spiritual overcomers who shine in contrast to the darkness of deception.

Conclusion: A Story of Triumph, Not Terror

In Revelation 12, we do not merely witness conflict—we behold conquest.

The Dragon is cast down.

The Child is exalted.

The saints are secure.

And the story of redemption, written in the stars and sung by the heavens, continues in the Church today. What began in a manger, was caught up in baptism, what was tested in the wilderness, and was finished on the cross is now proclaimed in the heavens:

Salvation belongs to the Lamb.

His Kingdom has come.

And the gates of hell shall not prevail against it.

Key Takeaways:

The Dragon represents Satan, the great adversary, whose power is real but ultimately superseded by God's divine purpose and Christ's triumph.

The "war in heaven" signifies a decisive spiritual victory secured by Jesus during His ministry, culminating in His ascension, where Satan was "cast out" from his position as accuser.

The Woman (faithful Israel) and the Child (Jesus) represent the redemptive plan culminating in Christ, whose victory over the Dragon in the wilderness and at the Cross affirmed His authority and secured the Church's preservation.

Chapter 6

SEALS, TRUMPHETS, AND BOWLS: DIVINE JUDGMENTS

The Scroll Unsealed: Unfolding of Divine Purpose

The Book of Revelation presents a profound and unified vision of divine judgment and redemption, symbolized through the sequential unfolding of seals, the sounding of trumpets, and the pouring out of bowls. These are not isolated events or disconnected calamities; they represent the progression of God's redemptive plan through Jesus Christ.

This pattern of divine judgment is not without precedent.

In Deuteronomy 28:60 God warned Israel, "Moreover he will bring upon thee all the diseases of Egypt, which thou wast afraid of; and they shall cleave unto thee," clearly indicating that if Israel turned to other gods, they would suffer the same plagues that once fell on Egypt.

This warning wasn't symbolic—it was covenantal.

Further, in Deuteronomy 29:24–25, God declared that when devastation fell upon the land, the nations would ask, "Wherefore hath the Lord done thus unto this land?.

Because they have forsaken the covenant of the Lord God of their fathers." These verses provide the spiritual and legal framework behind the judgments seen in Revelation.

The trumpet and bowl judgments are not futuristic horrors—they are the rightful consequences of covenant violation, mirroring the same plagues once reserved for Egypt, now turned upon Jerusalem for its idolatry.

At the heart of this progression stands the sealed scroll introduced in Revelation 5—held in the hand of God and received by the Lamb who was slain and now lives.

This scroll is not simply a record of future disasters; it is the Revelation itself.

The scroll is described as "written within and on the backside" (Revelation 5:1), a detail rich in covenantal symbolism. This dual inscription signifies the totality of God's redemptive plan encompassing both the Old and New Covenants. The writing on the backside represents the Old Covenant, externally inscribed on tablets of stone and administered through law, sacrifice, and temple. The writing within reflects the New Covenant, written on the hearts of believers through the Spirit, fulfilling what the law foreshadowed. Together, they signify that the scroll contains the entire redemptive narrative, culminating in Christ's finished work. Only the Lamb—who fulfilled the Old and inaugurated the New—is worthy to open such a scroll.

As declared in Revelation 1:1, "The Revelation of Jesus Christ, which God gave unto Him," so in Revelation 5 we witness that divine transfer.

The Lamb, freshly risen and glorified, is declared worthy to receive and reveal what was previously hidden.

Each seal broken by the Lamb marks another stage in that revealing—truths and judgments once concealed are now made known to His servants through the Spirit.

The seals, then, represent more than ominous warnings; they are the initial stages of divine revelation and judgment, particularly directed toward Israel and Jerusalem.

If we consider Jesus' Olivet Discourse as a reflection on spiritual realities already set in motion, the breaking of these seals corresponds to covenantal judgments that began unfolding in Israel's history, culminated through the ministry of John the Baptist (the final trumpet of warning), and culminated in the final outpouring of wrath seen in the bowls.

From the entry of Jesus into Jerusalem to the cross, each stage reveals the transition from the old covenant to the new, exposing apostasy and heralding redemption.

This chapter will trace that spiritual progression, showing how the seals initiate the Revelation's message, the trumpets amplify it as warnings, and the bowls complete it in covenantal judgment and purifying fire.

A Prophetic Parallel from Zechariah

This vision of the four horsemen is strikingly paralleled in Zechariah 6, where four chariots emerge from between two mountains of brass—each pulled by colored horses nearly identical to those in Revelation. These are called "the four spirits of the heavens" (Zechariah 6:5), sent forth by God to walk to and fro through the earth, demonstrating divine oversight and judgment. Just as the horsemen in Revelation symbolize spiritual forces unleashed by Christ, Zechariah's chariots reflect heavenly agents executing God's purposes across the earth.

The alignment of horse colors—red, black, white, and grisled—confirms that Revelation is echoing Zechariah's imagery, but through the lens of covenantal judgment. These are not global disasters as often interpreted, but spiritual judgments against the old covenant system, unfolding under Christ's authority.

Following this vision, Zechariah records the crowning of Joshua the high priest, a prophetic image of the coming Messiah who "shall build the temple of the Lord...and shall sit and rule upon his throne" (Zechariah 6:12–13). This points forward to Jesus, the true Branch, who is both priest and king.

In this light, the opening of the seals and the sending forth of the four riders is not merely an unfolding of judgment, but a divine enthronement sequence. Christ, crowned and seated, sends forth spiritual decrees that dismantle the old covenant order and establish the kingdom of God through His people.

The Breaking of the Seals: A Spiritual Prelude to Christ's Unveiling

Each seal broken by the Lamb represents not just judgment, but revelation. These are not random events—they are divine decrees unraveling the Old Covenant order. Only through this unraveling can the full unveiling of Christ take place. As the old is judged and dismantled, the new emerges. The scroll, held in the Father's hand, contains the consummated redemptive plan of God. Christ does not merely observe its opening—He initiates and fulfills it.

The seals do not merely precede Christ's reign—they prepare the way for it. Every horseman sent, every soul crying out, every celestial disturbance, signals the closing of the Old Covenant age and the inauguration of Christ's kingdom.

The First Seal: The White Horse and Its Rider (Revelation 6:1–2)

The first seal reveals a rider on a white horse, symbolizing conquest and deception.

This figure parallels Jesus' warning in the Olivet Discourse about false Christs who would deceive many (Matthew 24:4–5).

Spiritually, this seal represents the various false messianic movements and spiritual deceptions that plagued Israel throughout its history, particularly during periods of exile and foreign domination.

These movements, often led by figures promising deliverance, drew the people further away from God's truth.

The Second Seal: The Red Horse and War (Revelation 6:3–4)

The second seal introduces a rider on a red horse, symbolizing war and conflict.

This aligns with Jesus' prediction of wars and rumors of wars (Matthew 24:6–7).

This seal represents the numerous wars and internal conflicts that Israel experienced, such as the Assyrian and Babylonian invasions, which were seen as divine judgments for their unfaithfulness.

These historical conflicts, characterized by strife and bloodshed, can be seen as precursors to the more intense spiritual judgments that would lead to the spiritual destruction of Jerusalem.

The Third Seal: The Black Horse and Famine (Revelation 6:5–6)

The third seal reveals a rider on a black horse, symbolizing famine.

Jesus warned that famines would be a sign of the beginning of sorrows (Matthew 24:7).

Spiritually, this seal represents periods of severe spiritual drought in Israel's history, where the people were deprived of prophetic voices and divine guidance.

This spiritual famine is reminiscent of the time between the last Old Testament prophets and the coming of John the Baptist, a period often referred to as the "silent years" when prophetic revelation was scarce.

The Fourth Seal: The Pale Horse and Death (Revelation 6:7–8)

The fourth seal brings forth a rider on a pale horse, representing death, followed by Hades, the grave.

This seal symbolizes the widespread death and devastation that occurred during significant periods of judgment in Israel's history, such as the fall of Samaria and Jerusalem.

The spiritual death accompanying Israel's persistent idolatry and rejection of God's covenant is vividly depicted in the prophetic writings, where Israel is often portrayed as a nation under the shadow of death, awaiting divine judgment.

The Fifth Seal: The Cry of the Martyrs (Revelation 6:9–11)

The fifth seal shifts the focus to the cry of the martyrs, those who had been faithful to God but suffered persecution and death.

This seal reflects the prophets and righteous individuals throughout Israel's history who were martyred for their commitment to God's truth.

The cry of these martyrs is a plea for divine justice, echoing the laments of prophets like Elijah and Jeremiah, who grieved over the nation's apostasy and called for God's intervention.

Their cry finds its answer in the ministry of John the Baptist, who, as the last of the Old Testament prophets, called Israel to repentance and warned of imminent judgment.

The Sixth Seal: Cosmic Disturbances (Revelation 6:12–17)

The sixth seal unveils cosmic disturbances—earthquakes, a darkened sun, and a blood-red moon—symbolizing the upheaval of the established order. These events represent the spiritual and political shifts that took place in Israel's history, particularly during times of exile and foreign domination.

The imagery also is linked to the prophetic descriptions of the Day of the Lord, a time of divine intervention and judgment anticipated in the Old Testament. Jesus, in the Olivet Discourse, mirrored these same signs as spiritual symbols of covenantal judgment.

"Immediately after the tribulation of those days shall the sun be darkened, and the moon shall not give her light, and the stars shall fall from heaven, and the powers of the heavens shall be shaken:

And then shall appear the sign of the Son of man in heaven: and then shall all the tribes of the earth mourn, and they shall see the Son of man coming in the clouds of heaven with power and great glory."—Matthew 24:29–30

This passage directly parallels the sixth seal's language:

"And I beheld when he had opened the sixth seal, and, lo, there was a great earthquake; and the sun became black as sackcloth of hair, and the moon became as blood;

And the stars of heaven fell unto the earth…"—Revelation 6:12–13

Just as the Old Testament prophets warned of the coming "Day of the Lord" with the piercing question, "Who can abide it?" (Joel 2:11; Malachi 3:2), Revelation echoes this solemn refrain in the opening of the sixth seal: "For the great day of his wrath is come; and who shall be able to stand?" (Revelation 6:17). This is not merely poetic coincidence—it is theological continuity. The same God who warned Israel through the prophets now reveals His judgment through the Lamb. The cry in Revelation is not the voice of pagan nations, but of covenantal people facing the consequences of rejecting their Messiah. The "Day of the Lord" has arrived—not as a distant apocalypse, but as the culminating judgment upon the Old Covenant world, with Jesus, the Lamb, executing justice in righteousness. Who can stand before the Lamb's truth? Only those who have been redeemed by His blood and walk in the light of the New Covenant.

The cosmic imagery in both passages is not to be interpreted as literal astronomical events, but as prophetic language signifying massive spiritual and governmental upheaval. Just as the fall of earthly kingdoms was often described in terms of celestial disturbances by the prophets, so too does Revelation use these symbols to portray the collapse of the Old Covenant world and the rise of the New.

The Sealing of the 144,000 and the Great Multitude

As the narrative transitions to Revelation 7, we encounter a significant interlude in the unfolding of divine judgments.

Four angels are seen standing at the four corners of the earth, holding back the four winds of destruction.

This imagery parallels Jesus' warning in the Olivet Discourse about the angels gathering His elect from the four winds (Matthew 24:31).

The holding back of these winds signifies a temporary pause in judgment, symbolizing God's mercy and the sealing of His people before the final outpouring of wrath.

During this pause, 144,000 from the tribes of Israel are sealed, representing the faithful remnant preserved by God. This sealing is reminiscent of the marking of God's faithful in Ezekiel 9, where those who grieved over the sins of Jerusalem were marked for protection. The sealing ensures their security amidst the judgments that are about to unfold.

Following this, John witnesses a great multitude that no one could number, from every nation, tribe, people, and language, standing before the throne and the Lamb.

This multitude is clothed in white robes and holding palm branches, symbols of victory and righteousness.

These Gentiles, who have been grafted into the kingdom, are the fulfillment of the promise that the gospel would reach all nations (Matthew 24:14).

They have come out of the "great tribulation," the period of intense Old Testament judgment and purification that led to their inclusion in God's kingdom.

This vision echoes the prophetic promise given through Isaiah:

"Enlarge the place of thy tent, and let them stretch forth the curtains of thine habitations: spare not, lengthen thy cords, and strengthen thy stakes; For thou shalt break forth on the right hand. and on the left; and thy seed shall inherit the Gentiles, and make the desolate cities to be inhabited." (Isaiah 54:2–3)

The great multitude John sees is the very fulfillment of Isaiah's command to expand the tent—the inclusion of the Gentiles into the household of faith. The desolate cities are now filled with the redeemed. The cords have indeed been lengthened, and the tent of God's dwelling now includes every nation, tribe, and tongue.

Parallels with the Olivet Discourse: One Taken, One Left

The events described in Revelation 7 also resonate with Jesus' teaching about the end times in the Olivet Discourse, particularly the statement "one will be taken and the other left" (Matthew 24:40–41).

This phrase signifies the sudden and selective nature of judgment, where the righteous are preserved while others face destruction.

The sealing of the 144,000 and the appearance of the great multitude in heaven represent the gathering of the faithful, those "taken" to be with the Lord, in contrast to those "left" to face the consequences of rejecting God.

Remember, this is all spiritual in nature.

The great multitude that appears in heaven represents the fulfillment of the promise that God's salvation would extend beyond Israel to include all nations. This is a pivotal moment in the narrative, showing that the Gentiles, who were once "far off," are now brought near by the blood of Christ (Ephesians 2:13). The imagery of this diverse multitude, united in worship before the throne, reflects the inclusive nature of God's kingdom, where all who believe in Christ are granted eternal life.

The Fulfillment of the Gospel: Proclamation in the Past

In the Olivet Discourse, Jesus spoke of the Gospel being preached "in all the world for a witness unto all nations; and then shall the end come" (Matthew 24:14). When we examine it through the lens of Scripture, particularly in the context of Romans 10, we gain a different perspective.

Paul, in Romans 10:18 quotes Psalm 19:4 to illustrate that the message of the Old Testament prophets had already gone out to the ends of the earth: "But I say, Have they not heard? Yes verily, their sound went into all the earth, and their words unto the ends of the world." Paul is emphasizing that the voice of the prophets—the proclamation of God's Word—had already reached all nations.

This is not a prophecy of a future global mission but a reflection on the fulfillment of that mission in the past.

"Their line is gone out through all the earth, and their words to the end of the world." (Psalm 19:4)

When Jesus mentions the Gospel being preached to all nations in the Olivet Discourse, He is not predicting a future event but rather affirming what had already been accomplished through the ministry of the Old Testament prophets. The prophetic voice had echoed throughout the known world, preparing the way for the coming of Christ and the events that would unfold in His ministry and beyond.

This past fulfillment is crucial to understanding the timing and nature of the events described in Revelation. The judgments, the opening of the seals, and the sounding of the trumpets are not waiting for a future global evangelization to be completed; they are tied to what has already occurred. The Gospel, as proclaimed by the prophets, had reached its divinely intended audience, setting the stage for the end times as understood through the life of Christ.

By recognizing that the "ends of the earth" had already been reached according to Paul in Romans, we see that the eschatological events Jesus speaks of are not contingent on a future global mission but are instead rooted in the completion of the prophetic message in the past. This perspective shifts our understanding of Revelation from a future anticipation to a reflection on fulfilled prophecy.

The prophetic vision in Revelation 6 and 7 closely mirrors Jesus' own warnings in the Olivet Discourse, recorded in Matthew 24, Mark 13, and Luke 21.

These parallels are striking and deliberate, revealing a unified message of covenantal judgment and redemptive fulfillment.

Just as the first seals introduce false Christs, wars, famines, and pestilence, so too did Jesus warn that many would come in His name, that wars and rumors of wars would arise, and that famine, disease, and earthquakes would signal the beginning of sorrows.

The cry of the martyrs under the fifth seal echoes the prophets and others that were delivered up, afflicted, and killed for His name's sake.

The sixth seal unveils cosmic disturbances (darkened sun, falling stars, a shaking of the heavens)—imagery Jesus directly applies to the time "immediately after the tribulation of those days."

These parallels affirm that Revelation 6 and 7 are a visionary expansion of the very judgment Jesus foretold, not of global destruction to come, but of covenantal fulfillment already underway.

The Seventh Seal: The Awe of the Revelation

When the Lamb opened the seventh seal, silence filled heaven—not as a pause in destruction, but as a holy hush before the most sacred unsealing. The scroll was no longer sealed. The mystery was now being made known.

"And when he had opened the seventh seal, there was silence in heaven about the space of half an hour." (Revelation 8:1)

This was not a moment of confusion or suspense—it was reverent awe, for what had long been concealed was now revealed. The scroll, written within and on the backside (Revelation 5:1), was now fully opened. What had been seen only in prophetic fragments throughout the ages was now complete. The Revelation of Jesus Christ had been unsealed.

"The Revelation of Jesus Christ, which God gave unto him, to show unto his servants things which must shortly come to pass…." (Revelation 1:1)

This divine flow of revelation follows a heavenly chain of glory:

God the Father gives the Revelation to Jesus Christ.

Jesus, the Lamb slain and now risen, receives the sealed scroll in Revelation 5:

"And he came and took the book out of the right hand of him that sat upon the throne." (Revelation 5:7)

Jesus then gives this Revelation to His servant John, to be shown to His servants. The Lamb who received the sealed scroll now gives voice to its contents—unfolding judgments, promises, and triumphs.

This is not a disconnected series of visions, but the opening of a single scroll—The Revelation of Jesus Christ Himself. Once the seventh seal is broken, we are witnessing the contents of the very book that was once sealed.

The trumpets, bowls, visions, and declarations are not separate scrolls, but part of the same divine narrative. The silence marks the threshold—the moment the scroll is now laid open in full, and its spiritual revelations begin to flow like thunder through history.

Here, the Old Covenant shadows end, and the full radiance of Christ's redemptive work emerges. No longer do we see in part. The mystery hidden from ages and generations is now fully declared.

"Having made known unto us the mystery of his will, according to his good pleasure which he hath purposed in himself." (Ephesians 1:9)

"Even the mystery which hath been hid from ages and from generations, but now is made manifest to his saints." (Colossians 1:26)

The scroll has been opened. The silence breaks. The Revelation of Jesus Christ, once sealed, now flows to His people through John and the Spirit.

And what follows is not destruction—but a deeper understanding of the Lamb, His triumph, His judgments, and His everlasting Kingdom.

The Trumpet Judgments: Warnings Leading to the Baptism of Jesus

The trumpet judgments in Revelation serve as divine warnings that mirror the plagues of Egypt but focus on the spiritual consequences for Israel.

These judgments are closely tied to the ministry of John the Baptist, who, like Moses, served as a herald of impending judgment.

John the Baptist was the prophetic voice crying in the wilderness, preparing the way for the Lord (Isaiah 40:3; Matthew 3:3).

His message was clear: "Repent, for the kingdom of heaven is at hand" (Matthew 3:2).

John's call to repentance was a spiritual trumpet blast, urging the people of Israel to turn back to God and avoid impending judgment.

John's message was not only a call to individual repentance but also a national call to Israel to return to their covenant with God.

His baptism of repentance symbolized the washing away of sins and a preparation for the coming of the Messiah.

The last words of the Old Testament, found in Malachi, prophesied that God would send Elijah the prophet before the "great and terrible day of the Lord" (Malachi 4:5).

Jesus explicitly identified John the Baptist as the fulfillment of this prophecy, confirming that John was the Elijah who was to come.

"And his disciples asked him, saying, Why then say the scribes that Elias must first come?

And Jesus answered and said unto them, Elias truly shall first come, and restore all things.

But I say unto you, That Elias is come already, and they knew him not, but have done unto him whatsoever they listed. Likewise shall also the Son of man suffer of them.

Then the disciples understood that he spake unto them of John the Baptist." (Matthew 17:10–13)

The identification of John with Elijah underscores the continuity between the Old and New Testaments.

Just as Elijah confronted the idolatry and apostasy of Israel, John confronted the spiritual decay of his generation, calling them to repentance and preparation for the Messiah.

John the Baptist stands as the final and greatest prophet of the Old Covenant, embodying both the Law (represented by Moses) and the Prophets (represented by Elijah).

His ministry marks the culmination of the Old Testament witness and the beginning of the New Covenant era.

John's role as the "bridge" between the Old and New Covenants highlights the significance of his ministry in the divine plan of redemption.

He represents the fulfillment of the Law and the Prophets, and his message sets the stage for the arrival of the Messiah.

In his fiery sermons, John warned of the wrath to come, likening the people to a "generation of vipers" and urging them to produce "fruits worthy of repentance" (Luke 3:7–9).

He declared that "And now also the axe is laid unto the root of the trees" (Matthew 3:10), signifying that judgment was imminent and that the people needed to repent before it was too late.

John's message was a stark warning that the time for repentance was short, and that failure to respond would result in judgment.

His imagery of the axe at the root of the trees conveys the urgency of the situation and the finality of the judgment that was about to come.

The trumpet judgments, therefore, represent the consequences of Israel's failure to heed the warnings of John the Baptist, leading to the eventual revelation of Jesus as the Messiah at His baptism.

First Trumpet: Hail and Fire Mixed with Blood (Revelation 8:7)

Parallel with the Plague of Hail and Fire (Exodus 9:23–24): The first trumpet judgment mirrors the plague of hail mixed with fire that struck Egypt.

In Revelation, hail, and fire mingled with blood are cast upon the earth, burning up a third of the earth's vegetation.

This judgment symbolizes the destruction of spiritual fruitfulness among those who reject Christ, just as the hail and fire devastated Egypt's crops.

Second Trumpet: A Burning Mountain Cast into the Sea (Revelation 8:8–9)

Parallel with the Plague of Blood (Exodus 7:20–21): The second trumpet mirrors the first plague in Egypt, where the Nile turned to blood.

In Revelation, a great mountain burning with fire is cast into the sea, turning a third of it to blood.

This symbolizes the spiritual death and corruption that befall those who reject Christ, foreshadowing the destruction of Jerusalem.

The mountain represents a powerful kingdom or empire, and its fiery destruction signifies the downfall of a corrupt and idolatrous power.

The sea turning to blood recalls the judgment on Egypt, but in this context, it represents the judgment on a covenant-breaking Israel.

Third Trumpet: A Great Star Called Wormwood Falls (Revelation 8:10–11)

Parallel with the Bitterness from the Golden Calf Incident (Exodus 32:19–20): The third trumpet causes a great star named Wormwood to fall, turning a third of the waters bitter.

This bitterness reflects the internal decay and idolatry of those who have turned away from God.

The name "Wormwood" suggests poison and bitterness, symbolizing the spiritual and moral corruption that follows apostasy.

This plague of bitter waters also (Revelation 8:11) evokes the scene at Marah, where the Israelites encountered undrinkable bitter water after their deliverance (Exodus 15:23). Just as their journey began with a test of faith at Marah, Israel's rejection of their Messiah and clinging to the Old Covenant brought the bitter consequences of disobedience full circle.

Fourth Trumpet: A Third of the Sun, Moon, and Stars Struck (Revelation 8:12)

Parallel with the Plague of Darkness (Exodus 10:21–23): The fourth trumpet judgment mirrors the ninth plague, where darkness covered Egypt for three days.

This judgment represents the spiritual darkness that engulfs Israel, failing to recognize the light of Christ.

The darkening of a third of the sun, moon, and stars symbolizes a partial but significant obscuring of the light of truth.

It reflects the spiritual blindness of those who have rejected the Messiah and now walk in darkness.

This judgment also serves as a foreshadowing of the total darkness that will come upon those who persist in their rebellion against God.

Fifth Trumpet: Locusts from the Abyss (Revelation 9:1–12)

Parallel with the Plague of Locusts (Exodus 10:12–15): The fifth trumpet unleashes locusts from the abyss, tormenting those without God's seal.

This mirrors the plague of locusts in Egypt and symbolizes the spiritual torment of those who have rejected God.

The locusts in Revelation are described as having the appearance of horses prepared for battle, with crowns of gold and faces like human faces.

Their torment is not physical but spiritual, reflecting the inner agony of those who have turned away from the covenant.

113

The duration of their torment, "five months," may symbolize a limited but intense period of judgment, emphasizing the severity of the consequences of rebellion against God.

Sixth Trumpet: Release of the Four Angels Bound at the Euphrates (Revelation 9:13–21)

Parallel with the Plague of Death (Exodus 12:29–30): The sixth trumpet releases four angels leading to the death of a third of mankind, paralleling the final plague in Egypt—the death of the firstborn.

The Euphrates River, a significant boundary in biblical times, symbolizes the border between God's people and their enemies.

The release of these angels represents the unleashing of divine judgment, resulting in widespread death and destruction.

This judgment serves as a stark reminder of the consequences of rejecting God's covenant and the inevitability of divine retribution for unrepentant sin.

This judgment is not abstract. Revelation explicitly identifies the city under judgment:

"And their dead bodies shall lie in the street of the great city, which spiritually is called Sodom and Egypt, where also our Lord was crucified." (Revelation 11:8)

The city is Jerusalem, the very place where Christ was crucified. But spiritually, it is called Sodom, for its moral corruption, and Egypt, for its hardened rebellion against God's covenant. This verse powerfully affirms that Jerusalem had become Egypt in spirit—deserving of the very plagues once poured out on Pharaoh. It is the clear and prophetic declaration that apostate Israel had become indistinguishable from the ancient enemies of God, and thus bore the same judgment.

Seventh Trumpet: Culmination in the Baptism of Jesus

The seventh trumpet represents the divine announcement of the King— just as the heavens opened at Jesus' baptism and the Father declared, "This is my beloved Son," so too Revelation 11:15 declares, "The kingdoms of this world are become the kingdoms of our Lord and of His Christ." The seventh trumpet, like the final trumpet in Israel's festivals, signals royal enthronement and covenant establishment.

Only then does Revelation 12 unfold—revealing the spiritual conflict behind Christ's earthly ministry. The woman (Israel) gives birth to the Messiah; the dragon opposes Him; the child is caught up to God, reflecting both His triumph over temptation and His baptism.

The Bowl Judgments: Final Judgments on Jerusalem, Culminating at the Cross

The bowl judgments represent the final and most severe phase of divine judgment, specifically targeting Jerusalem. These judgments begin with Jesus' triumphal entry into Jerusalem and culminate in His crucifixion.

Jesus' entry into Jerusalem marked the beginning of the final week of His earthly ministry.

As He entered the city, the people shouted, "Hosanna to the Son of David!" recognizing Him as the Messiah (Matthew 21:9).

However, Jesus knew that Jerusalem would reject Him, and He wept over the city, "Saying, If thou hadst known, even thou, at least in this thy day, the things which belong unto thy peace! but now they are hid from thine eyes." (Luke 19:42)

This lament foreshadows the bowl judgments that would soon follow.

Jesus' entry into Jerusalem is also symbolic of the arrival of the king who comes in peace, but His peace is rejected, leading to the inevitable judgment.

Immediately after entering Jerusalem, Jesus cleansed the temple, driving out those who were buying and selling, "And said unto them, It is written, My house shall be called the house of prayer; but ye have made it a den of thieves." (Matthew 21:13)

This act of cleansing was both a prophetic sign of judgment against the corrupt religious system and a fulfillment of Malachi's prophecy that the Lord would come to His temple and purify it (Malachi 3:1–3).

The cleansing of the temple represents the purging of corruption and the reestablishment of true worship, but it also serves as a final warning to the religious leaders who have turned God's house into a place of commerce and exploitation.

Jesus cursed a barren fig tree on His way to Jerusalem, saying, "No man eat fruit of thee hereafter for ever …" (Mark 11:14).

This act symbolized the judgment on Jerusalem and the nation of Israel for their spiritual barrenness and rejection of the Messiah.

The fig tree, often a symbol of Israel in the Old Testament, represents the nation that has failed to produce the fruits of righteousness.

The cursing of the fig tree is a powerful symbol of the impending judgment on a people who have rejected their Messiah.

First Bowl: Sores on Those with the Mark of the Beast (Revelation 16:2)

Parallel also with the Plague of Boils (Exodus 9:8–11): The first bowl judgment brings painful sores on those who bear the seal of deception.

This parallels the plague of boils in Egypt, where painful sores afflicted the Egyptians.

In Revelation, this judgment symbolizes the spiritual afflictions that come upon those who reject Christ and align themselves with the corrupt religious and political system of Jerusalem.

The sores represent the internal corruption and guilt that manifest externally, indicating the moral and spiritual decay of those who have chosen to follow the beast rather than God.

Second Bowl: The Sea Turns to Blood (Revelation 16:3)

Parallel with the Plague of Blood (Exodus 7:20–21): The second bowl judgment turns the sea to blood, symbolizing the complete spiritual death that comes upon Jerusalem for rejecting Christ.

Just as the Nile turning to blood caused death and devastation in Egypt, this judgment represents the irreversible consequences of rejecting the Messiah.

The sea, often symbolic of the nations, turning to blood, indicates the widespread judgment that affects not only Jerusalem but also the surrounding regions.

This judgment emphasizes the severity of the consequences of covenantal unfaithfulness.

Third Bowl: Rivers and Springs Turn to Blood (Revelation 16:4–7)

Parallel with the Plague of Blood: Just as the waters of Egypt were turned to blood, so too are the rivers and springs in Revelation.

The angel of the waters declares God's righteousness, affirming that these judgments are just retribution for the shedding of the blood of saints and prophets.

This judgment symbolizes the complete corruption and spiritual death of those who have rejected God's offer of salvation through Christ.

The turning of all water sources to blood signifies the totality of the judgment, leaving no place untouched by the consequences of rejecting God.

The declaration of righteousness by the angel underscores the justice of God's judgments, emphasizing that they are deserved and proportionate to the sins committed.

Fourth Bowl: Scorching Heat from the Sun (Revelation 16:8–9)

Parallel also with the Plague of Fire and Hail (Exodus 9:23–24): The scorching heat from the sun in the fourth bowl symbolizes the intensity of God's wrath against Jerusalem.

This judgment mirrors the plagues of fire and hail that brought devastation to Egypt, now manifesting as a relentless, inescapable heat.

The people of Jerusalem, refusing to repent, are scorched by the heat, representing the overwhelming and consuming nature of God's judgment.

The scorching heat also symbolizes the burning anger of God against sin, and the people's refusal to repent despite the severity of the judgment highlights their hardened hearts and stubborn rebellion against God.

Fifth Bowl: Darkness over the Beast's Kingdom (Revelation 16:10–11)

Parallel again with the Plague of Darkness (Exodus 10:21–23): The plague of darkness that covered Egypt for three days is mirrored in the fifth bowl judgment, where darkness falls upon the kingdom of the beast.

This darkness symbolizes the spiritual blindness and anguish that engulf those who reject the light of Christ.

Just as Egypt was plunged into physical darkness, Jerusalem is plunged into spiritual darkness regarding the truth of the Messiah.

The darkness also represents the judgment on the corrupt religious and political systems that have opposed God, leading to their inevitable downfall.

Sixth Bowl: Drying Up of the Euphrates (Revelation 16:12)

Parallel with the Parting of the Red Sea: In Exodus, the parting of the Red Sea allowed Israel to escape from Egypt.

In Revelation, the drying up of the Euphrates prepares the way for the kings of the east, signaling the approach of final judgment upon Jerusalem.

This reversal of the Exodus miracle symbolizes that the land, once a place of deliverance, now becomes a place of judgment.

The drying up of the Euphrates also signifies the removal of barriers to invasion, allowing the spiritual forces of judgment to enter and bring about the destruction of the corrupt city.

This judgment emphasizes the inevitability of God's justice and the futility of resisting His will.

The Seventh Bowl: "It Is Done" and the Final Plague of Death of the Firstborn

The seventh bowl is poured into the air—the symbolic realm of spiritual dominion. A great voice resounds from the temple in heaven: "It is done." This proclamation marks the climactic moment of divine fulfillment, echoing the final words of Christ on the Cross: "It is finished."

This final plague corresponds with the last plague in Egypt—the death of the firstborn. In that ancient judgment, the firstborn of Egypt perished at midnight, and there was a great cry in the land. That moment broke Pharaoh's resistance and led to Israel's release from bondage. But in the greater fulfillment, it was not Egypt's firstborn who died—it was Israel's own Firstborn Son.

At Calvary, Jesus took upon Himself the full weight of judgment. He was the Passover Lamb and the Firstborn Son. His death was not merely an act of Roman brutality—it was the spiritual culmination of all the covenantal plagues, now falling not upon Egypt, but upon spiritual Israel. Just as the blood on the doorposts spared Israel's households, so the blood of Jesus now secures eternal deliverance for all who are under it.

When the voice declares "It is done", heaven affirms that justice has been satisfied and the covenantal transition is complete. This bowl does not introduce new destruction—it confirms that all has been fulfilled, and the old covenant world has reached its appointed end.

A great earthquake follows, similar to the time of the cross, symbolizing the irreversible shaking of the former system. The city—apostate Jerusalem—is split into three parts, representing total covenantal disintegration. Hailstones fall from heaven, bringing weighty judgment from above. These are not physical disasters but vivid spiritual images, echoing the plagues of Egypt and revealing the collapse of the law-based religious system that rejected its Messiah.

This judgment confirms what Jesus had already warned in His parable of the landowner: after the Son was killed, the tenants would be judged, and the vineyard given to others. That moment now arrives. The harlot is cast off, and the true Bride receives the inheritance.

In this way, the death of the Firstborn (Jesus) aligns with the seventh bowl, the final plague, and the closing of the old covenant age. The harlot, Jerusalem, is cast off, and the true Bride is revealed. The voice from heaven does not cry in despair—it announces victory: "It is done."

Conclusion

The seals, trumpets, and bowl judgments in Revelation are deeply interconnected, revealing the progressive unfolding of God's judgment upon Israel and Jerusalem.

These judgments are not mere historical events but represent the spiritual consequences of disobedience and the ultimate fulfillment of God's covenantal promises.

From the initial breaking of the seals to the final outpouring of the bowls, these judgments underscore the seriousness of rejecting God's truth and the mercy extended through Christ's redemptive work.

The narrative of Revelation thus reveals the profound depths of God's plan, where judgment and redemption are intricately woven together, leading to the establishment of the new covenant and the ultimate victory of Christ. By understanding the connections between the symbols of unfolding covenantal judgment, we gain a deeper appreciation of the continuity of God's plan and the fulfillment of His promises through Jesus Christ.

Reflections on Divine Judgment

As we've seen, the judgments of Revelation are not waiting to be unleashed—they have already poured out, fulfilling their purpose at the Cross. Yet, judgment still speaks. It reminds us that God is holy, that sin carries consequence, and that grace was bought at the greatest price.

These echoes from Egypt—and from Jerusalem—aren't just history. They call us to examine what we've built our lives upon. Have we heeded the trumpets? Have we stood under the blood of the Lamb?

The cross remains the dividing line between wrath and redemption. And for those in Christ, judgment has become the doorway to eternal peace.

Key Takeaways:

The Seals, Trumpets, and Bowls are not literal future global catastrophes, but symbolic representations of progressive divine judgments against Israel and Jerusalem, culminating in the transition from the Old to the New Covenant.

These judgments echo and fulfill the plagues God poured out on Egypt, demonstrating the consequences of covenant violation and apostasy.

The "Seventh Bowl" marks the climactic moment of divine fulfillment at the Cross, where Christ's "It is finished" signifies the end of the Old Covenant age and the establishment of eternal deliverance.

Chapter 7

SACRED FLAMES: THE SPIRIT'S PURIFYING WORK

Fire: Manifestation of the Cleansing Spirit

Throughout the annals of scripture, the divine narrative often employs the element of fire as a symbol of transformation, purification, and judgment.

Fire, a force both constructive and destructive, serves as a powerful metaphor for God's active presence and intervention in human history.

This chapter embarks on an illuminating exploration, inviting readers to uncover the profound connections between the Day of Pentecost in Acts 2, the apocalyptic vision in Revelation 20, and the prophetic imagery in Joel 2.

By examining these sacred texts, we will reveal a shared essence of fiery manifestations, divine judgments, and the overarching narrative that unites these events into a singular divine occurrence.

Through the lens of key scriptures, we will understand the significance of heavenly fire in the unfolding of God's eternal plan and how it relates to the broader themes of the book.

The Fiery Manifestation of Pentecost

Our journey begins with the Day of Pentecost, an event that occurred fifty days after the resurrection of Jesus. The disciples had gathered in Jerusalem during the Feast of Pentecost, anticipating the fulfillment of Jesus' promise—the outpouring of the Holy Spirit. This momentous event is pivotal in Christian history, marking the birth of the Church and the beginning of a new era in God's redemptive plan.

Acts 2:2–3 describes the dramatic arrival of the Holy Spirit: "And suddenly there came a sound from heaven as of a rushing mighty wind, and it filled all the house where they were sitting.

And there appeared unto them cloven tongues like as of fire, and it sat upon each of them." The "cloven tongues like as of fire" represent the Holy Spirit's descent, a symbol of purification and empowerment.

This fiery manifestation enabled the disciples to speak in various languages, breaking down barriers between nations and facilitating the spread of the Gospel.

The fire here symbolizes the transformative power of the Holy Spirit, purifying the disciples and equipping them for their mission.

It was a moment of awe and wonder, an unmistakable sign that God's Spirit was now actively working through His people. This divine encounter not only empowered the disciples but also demonstrated to all present that God's presence was now accessible to everyone.

The Fiery Judgment of Revelation 20: Shifting our focus to Revelation

Revelation 20:9 provides a striking image: "And they went up on the breadth of the earth, and compassed the camp of the saints about, and the beloved city: and fire came down from God out of heaven, and devoured them." The "fire from heaven" signifies divine judgment, purging the world of evil.

It is crucial to understand that this fiery judgment is preceded by the spiritual transformation of the saints, paralleling the disciples' empowerment on Pentecost.

This connection highlights a recurring theme: fire as an agent of divine purification and empowerment. Just as the disciples were empowered by the Holy Spirit to fulfill their mission, the saints in Revelation are prepared to usher in God's kingdom. Both events emphasize the transformative power of divine fire and the fulfillment of God's redemptive plan.

Moreover, considering various theological perspectives on these texts adds depth. Some scholars view Revelation's fire as a literal event, a future occurrence that will physically purify the earth. Others interpret it metaphorically, symbolizing the ultimate triumph of good over evil. By exploring these interpretations, we can appreciate the richness of the biblical narrative and its multifaceted implications for believers.

The Prophetic Fire of Joel 2

To deepen our understanding, we turn to Joel 2, a prophetic text that profoundly influenced the interpretation of Pentecost and Revelation 20.

Joel's prophecy in Joel 2:28–29 foretells a significant outpouring of the Spirit: "And it shall come to pass afterward, that I will pour out my spirit upon all flesh; and your sons and your daughters shall prophesy, your old men shall dream dreams, your young men shall see visions: And also upon the servants and upon the handmaids in those days will I pour out my spirit."

Joel's prophecy envisions a universal outpouring of the Spirit, transcending age, gender, and social status. This vision finds fulfillment on the Day of Pentecost when the Holy Spirit descends upon the disciples, empowering them to prophesy and communicate with diverse nations. The fire in Joel's prophecy symbolizes the purifying and transformative power of the Holy Spirit, aligning with the imagery in Acts 2 and Revelation 20.

Imagine the hope and excitement this prophecy must have stirred in its original audience. Joel's words promised a future where God's Spirit would be accessible to all people, not just a select few. This democratization of the divine presence was revolutionary, heralding a new era of inclusivity and spiritual empowerment.

Moreover, Joel's emphasis on the Spirit's outpouring parallels the fire's role in Acts and Revelation. The Holy Spirit's descent is not merely about communication but also about spiritual renewal and empowerment. This theme of fire as a purifying force underscores the continuity of God's transformative work across different scriptural events.

Exploring how different theological traditions interpret Joel's prophecy further enriches our understanding. Some view it as a prelude to the eschatological fulfillment seen in Revelation, where the Spirit's outpouring will culminate in the final purification and renewal of all creation. Others see it as a continual process, with each generation experiencing the Spirit's transformative power anew.

The Converging Fires: Judgment and Redemption

In the final segment of our exploration, we draw parallels between the consuming fire in Revelation 20 and the conversion of 3000 souls on the Day of Pentecost in Acts 2.

Revelation 20:9 describes the fire that descends from heaven and consumes those surrounding the city, symbolizing divine judgment and purification.

This imagery connects with the mass conversion on Pentecost, where Peter's sermon led to the conversion of 3000 individuals (Acts 2:4).

This conversion signifies the transformative power of the Holy Spirit, as foretold by Joel and symbolized by the fiery tongues.

The fire in Revelation 20 serves as an agent of divine judgment, preparing the world for renewal. Similarly, the fiery tongues on Pentecost represent the Holy Spirit's purifying work, transforming individuals and enabling them to participate in God's mission. Both instances highlight the dual role of fire in judgment and redemption, emphasizing the transformative power of the Holy Spirit.

Consider the metaphorical fire that refines precious metals, burning away impurities and leaving behind something pure and valuable. In the same way, God's fire purifies and transforms, preparing individuals and communities for His divine purposes. The fiery judgment in Revelation ensures that only what is pure remains, just as the fire on Pentecost enabled a purified and empowered community to emerge.

The Final Fire: Death, Hades, and the Consuming Flame of Fulfillment

If fire in Scripture is God's purifying agent—not merely punitive, but redemptive—then the lake of fire can be understood not as the eternal torture chamber of tradition, but as the consummation of divine justice, the final cleansing of everything incompatible with Christ's life. Revelation 20:14 proclaims, "And death and hell were cast into the lake of fire. This is the second death." Notice what is judged here: not merely individual souls, but death itself and Hades, the grave. This is not a literal physical place, but a spiritual conclusion—a burning away of all that once ruled under the Old Covenant. The Spirit's fire, which purifies the saints, now consumes the last remnants of sin's reign: death, law, and condemnation. What is not written in the Book of Life—what is not found in Christ—is destroyed. This interpretation suggests it is not about flesh being burned in literal flames, but about the end of separation, the end of legal judgment, and "The last enemy that shall be destroyed is death." (1 Cor. 15:26).

The 'second death' in this context is not primarily about individuals, but about the system that stood against the Spirit's work. It is the divine cleansing fire poured out on the old order. Those who worship the beast find no rest, as they have not entered into Christ's rest. This spiritual torment, where the smoke of their torment goes up forever and ever, is a consequence of clinging to legalism and rejecting the grace of Christ. Because of Christ, Satan has no power over the Christian, and the beast has no dominion over those who walk by grace. With death and the grave consumed, the path is fully open for the New Jerusalem to shine in unending light.

Conclusion: The Eternal Symphony of Divine Fire

In conclusion, our journey through the Day of Pentecost, Revelation 20, and Joel 2 reveals the unity of divine fire and transformation in God's eternal plan. These interconnected events demonstrate the continuous work of God's transformative fire, from the birth of the Church on Pentecost to the final judgment and renewal in Revelation. Joel's prophecy underscores the universal nature of this divine event, portraying a vision realized in Acts 2 and culminating in Revelation 20.

The fiery judgment in Revelation and the conversion on Pentecost both exemplify the Holy Spirit's transformative power, whether through purification or redemption. These parallel narratives illustrate God's overarching plan for humanity's purification and empowerment through the Holy Spirit's fire. The Day of Pentecost, Revelation 20, and Joel 2 serve as a testament to the unity of God's redemptive work, reinforcing the eternal nature of His divine plan.

As we reflect on these scriptures, let us embrace the purifying fire of the Holy Spirit in our own lives. Let us be open to His transformative power, allowing it to refine us, empower us, and guide us as we participate in God's ongoing work of redemption and renewal. Through the fire of the Holy Spirit, we can be instruments of God's love and justice in the world, shining brightly with the light of His presence.

Key Takeaways:

Fire in Scripture is a multifaceted symbol of God's transformative presence, representing both purification and judgment.

The fiery manifestation at Pentecost symbolizes the Holy Spirit's purifying and empowering work, marking the birth of the Church and a new era of spiritual accessibility.

The "lake of fire" in Revelation symbolizes the ultimate consumption of all that is incompatible with Christ's life—including death, law, and condemnation—rather than an eternal torture chamber.

Chapter 8

UNMASKING THE DECEPTION: LEGALISM AND IDOLATRY

The Beast: Legalism vs. Grace

Revelation 13 presents one of the most compelling and symbolically rich chapters in the Bible. It describes a beast rising from the sea, embodying traits of the four beasts from Daniel 7. This chapter delves into the intricate symbolism of the beast, its connections to the Law, and how these images illustrate the spiritual struggles between law-based righteousness and faith-based grace. The beast rises as a spiritual system of legalism immediately following Christ's baptism and anointing (Revelation 12:5–13), standing in opposition to the grace and truth brought by the Lamb.

Revelation 13:1–2 Sets the Stage

"And I stood upon the sand of the sea and saw a beast rise up out of the sea, having seven heads and ten horns, and upon his horns ten crowns, and upon his heads the name of blasphemy. And the beast which I saw was like unto a leopard, and his feet were as the feet of a bear, and his mouth as the mouth of a lion: and the dragon gave him his power, and his seat, and great authority." (Revelation 13:1–2)

Parallels with Daniel's Beasts

The composite beast of Revelation 13 integrates the typological power structures of Daniel but is repurposed to portray the totality of the legal system of the Old Covenant. It is the Law in weakness, clothed in authority, but absent of Spirit. This Law-based system mimics the spiritual attributes of the physical kingdoms of the beasts of Daniel.

Lion with Eagle's Wings (Daniel 7:4): Represents Babylon, indicating a period of strength and subsequent humbling. The beast's mouth like a lion symbolizes authoritative and fearsome power.

Bear (Daniel 7:5): Represents Medo-Persia, known for its strength and conquests. The beast's feet like a bear signify its crushing power.

Leopard (Daniel 7:6): Represents Greece under Alexander the Great, characterized by swift conquests. The body of the beast like a leopard indicates agility and pervasive influence.

Dreadful and Terrible Beast (Daniel 7:7): Represents Rome, known for its iron strength and harsh rule. The ten horns with crowns symbolize earthly domination and the pervasive reach of this beast's power.

The Law as the Deceptive Beast

The seven heads and ten horns of the beast symbolize aspects of the Mosaic Law and the religious system that relied on works for righteousness. This beast stands as the spiritual embodiment of the old covenant system. One that includes not only priesthood, sacrifice, and temple, but also cycles with works-based allegiance.

The beast is the works-based system of salvation—centered in temple worship, law adherence, and priesthood performance.

Galatians 3:10–13 provides crucial insights: "For as many as are of the works of the law are under the curse: for it is written, Cursed is every one that continueth not in all things which are written in the book of the law to do them.

But that no man is justified by the law in the sight of God, it is evident: for, The just shall live by faith.

And the law is not of faith: but, The man that doeth them shall live in them.

Christ hath redeemed us from the curse of the law, being made a curse for us: for it is written, Cursed is every one that hangeth on a tree."

This passage highlights the curse of relying on the Law for justification. The Law demands perfect obedience, which no human can achieve, leading to spiritual bondage and torment.

Romans 7:9–11 and 24–25 further explains the inner conflict: "For I was alive without the law once: but when the commandment came, sin revived, and I died.

And the commandment, which was ordained to life, I found to be unto death.

For sin, taking occasion by the commandment, deceived me, and by it slew me.

O wretched man that I am! who shall deliver me from the body of this death? I thank God through Jesus Christ our Lord.

So then with the mind I myself serve the law of God; but with the flesh the law of sin."

Paul's struggle illustrates the torment of trying to achieve righteousness through the Law, which ultimately leads to a sense of spiritual death and wretchedness.

Three Beasts and the Crowns: A Counterfeit Kingdom

Revelation presents three terrifying figures: the dragon, the beast from the sea, and the scarlet beast of Revelation 17. At first glance, they may appear as disconnected monsters, but spiritually they are interconnected.

Their crowns reveal their nature. The dragon bears seven crowns upon its heads (Revelation 12:3) symbolizing spiritual power and dominion through deception—a counterfeit of divine authority. The beast from the sea, however, bears ten crowns on its horns (Revelation 13:1) representing earthly power, kingship, and institutional force—law, government, and even systems co-opted to enforce the dragon's agenda.

Then comes the scarlet beast of Revelation 17: it bears no crowns—only seven heads and ten horns. This final form is stripped of pretense. No crowns remain because its power is exposed for what it is—sin itself. This beast is ridden by the harlot—apostate Jerusalem—and represents the naked corruption that once masqueraded as divine.

The three stages of the beast form a spiritual progression:

Dragon (Revelation 12) – Satan and spiritual authority through deception

Beast from the Sea (Revelation 13) – Old Covenant legalism absent faith and grace

Scarlet Beast (Revelation 17) – Sin exposed, revealed without crowns or pretense

Through these beasts, Satan mimics God's kingdom—but his mimicry is ultimately unmasked by the Lamb.

The False Prophet

Revelation 13:11 introduces another beast:

"And I beheld another beast coming up out of the earth; and he had two horns like a lamb, and he spake as a dragon." (Revelation 13:11)

This second beast, the false prophet, represents religious authorities who mislead the people. The imagery of "two horns like a lamb" suggests a deceptive appearance of innocence and piety, while "speaking as a dragon" reveals its true nature of deceit and evil.

The false prophet is not merely religious deception in general but specifically the high priesthood—who enforced temple worship after Christ and led the people into trusting the Law instead of the Lamb. This religious leadership upheld and enforced the legalistic system, leading people away from the truth of salvation through faith in Christ.

The Second Beast – Deception Masquerading as Righteousness

If the first beast represents a system of outward power built on legalism and covenantal rejection, then the second beast arises as its insidious accomplice—a false prophet that enforces deception in the name of holiness. Revelation 13:11 describes this second beast as having "two horns like a lamb," yet speaking "as a dragon." Outwardly, it appears gentle and Christlike—like the Lamb—but its voice reveals its allegiance.

This is the face of religious deception cloaked in piety. It is the seduction of false prophets who mimic spiritual authority but betray the truth. This beast exercises all the power of the first before it, compelling the earth to worship the beastly system of law and works-based righteousness.

Just as the Pharisees exalted the law while rejecting the Lawgiver, the second beast points not to Christ but back to the legal structure that Christ fulfilled. It produces counterfeit signs, seeks to mimic the Spirit's power, and ultimately persuades men to accept a false gospel rooted in human effort.

In this context, the second beast symbolizes the high priest—man's attempt to enforce righteousness without regeneration, authority without the Spirit, and worship without truth. It is the voice of manipulation, performance, and fear disguised as devotion.

Together, these two beasts—the religious law-system (the first beast) and false spiritual authority of the high priest (the second)—form a seductive yet strict deceptive allegiance to the Law. The dragon gives power to the beast, the beast establishes dominion, and the false prophet leads people into allegiance with this deception.

It is no coincidence that this second beast is later called the false prophet (Revelation 19:20) for its mission is to lead people away from Christ while appearing to speak for God. It is the spiritual voice of apostate religion and its legalistic control, led by the High Priest of the Old Covenant.

The Image of the Beast and Idolatry

Revelation 13:14–15 Describes the creation and worship of the beast's image:

"And deceiveth them that dwell on the earth by the means of those miracles which he had power to do in the sight of the beast; saying to them that dwell on the earth, that they should make an image to the beast, which had the wound by a sword, and did live. And he had power to give life unto the image of the beast, that the image of the beast should both speak, and cause that as many as would not worship the image of the beast should be killed." (Revelation 13:14–15)

This declaration restores clarity—reminding us that life, judgment, wounding, and healing belong to God alone.

This passage symbolizes deeper spiritual idolatry and corruption. The image of the beast represents the temple and the religious system that demands absolute allegiance, mirroring historical periods of apostasy in Israel.

The temple became the image—a magnificent structure that looked holy, but after Christ's atonement, was emptied of glory and filled with dead works.

Herod's temple, in particular, fits this symbolism. Rebuilt by a Roman-appointed king and praised for its beauty, it became the central object of religious allegiance even after the veil was torn. Though modeled after Solomon's temple, it became a gilded shell—a political and religious image that drew the people back under bondage.

"For as many as are of the works of the law are under the curse…"
(Galatians 3:10)
"For they being ignorant of God's righteousness… have not submitted themselves unto the righteousness of God." (Romans 10:3)
"But now, after that ye have known God… how turn ye again to the weak and beggarly elements…" (Galatians 4:9)

It appeared holy but was used by the beast system to enforce worship of the Law after grace had already come. Thus, Herod's temple stood not as a house of God, but as the very image of the beast—an idol of false sanctity, animated by priestly power yet destined for judgment.

The Mark of the Beast

Revelation 13:16–17 Signifies Allegiance to This Apostate System:

"And he causeth all, both small and great, rich, and poor, free and bond, to receive a mark in their right hand, or in their foreheads: And that no man might buy or sell, save he that had the mark, or the name of the beast, or the number of his name." (Revelation 13:16–17)

This mark contrasts with the commandment in Deuteronomy 6:6–8 to bind the Law as a sign on one's hand and forehead, indicating complete devotion to God: "And these words, which I command thee this day, shall be in thine heart: And thou shalt teach them diligently unto thy children, and shalt talk of them when thou sittest in thine house, and when thou walkest by the way, and when thou liest down, and when thou risest up.

And thou shalt bind them for a sign upon thine hand, and they shall be as frontlets between thine eyes."

The mark is not about commerce or future tech; it is a spiritual badge of allegiance to the Law after grace had come—the identity of those who cling to the old covenant system for righteousness.

This is the system behind the mark—one that operates by exclusion. No one may 'buy or sell' unless they carry the identification of this beast. In other words, one cannot participate in the system spiritually without compromise and submission. It is not about trade or economics, but about access and allegiance. In striking contrast, Proverbs 23:23 urges, "Buy the truth, and sell it not"—highlighting a spiritual economy where truth is acquired through surrender, not submission to corrupt systems. The phrase 'buy or sell' is symbolic of participation and validation in the covenantal economy.

The seal of deception symbolizes a perverse counterpart, representing total commitment to a system of works and legalism rather than faith. This deception leads individuals away from the truth that salvation comes through grace and faith in Jesus Christ.

This spiritual torment is not just figurative—it is echoed again in Revelation 14, where the result of clinging to the beast is vividly described.

Revelation 14:11 solemnly warns, "And the smoke of their torment ascendeth up for ever and ever: and they have no rest day nor night, who worship the beast and his image."

This haunting truth perfectly aligns with the spiritual burden of legalism. Those who cling to the Law, rejecting the grace of Christ, experience no spiritual rest—only the constant striving of self-justification and the torment of never being good enough.

Hebrews 4:9 declares, "There remaineth therefore a rest to the people of God." But this rest is reserved for those who trust in Christ's finished work, not those who continue worshipping the image of the beast—the temple, the Law, and the legalistic system.

A Mark or a Seal: Accept the Grace Through Faith

Believers now bear a different mark:

Ephesians 1:13: "...after that ye believed, ye were sealed with that holy Spirit of promise."

The seal of the Spirit marks those who rest in Christ, while the mark of the beast marks those still striving under the Law.

Rejected Fire: The Absence of God's Approval

In the days of Moses and Solomon, fire came down from heaven to ignite the altar (Leviticus 9:24; 2 Chronicles 7:1), signifying God's approval of the tabernacle and temple. But after the cross, that fire never came again. Christ's sacrifice was the final offering.

To continue temple rituals after Calvary was to offer strange fire—a worship God no longer accepted. As Ezekiel 10:18 states: "Then the glory of the Lord departed from off the threshold of the house."

This is why 666 is a parody of atonement: a high priest with no fire, a temple with no glory, and a law that can no longer justify.

Faith and Grace vs. Works and Law

The New Testament consistently contrasts the futility of the Law with the sufficiency of faith and grace.

Romans 3:20–22: "Therefore by the deeds of the law there shall no flesh be justified in his sight: for by the law is the knowledge of sin. But now the righteousness of God without the law is manifested, being witnessed by the law and the prophets; Even the righteousness of God which is by faith of Jesus Christ unto all and upon all them that believe: for there is no difference."

Galatians 2:16: "Knowing that a man is not justified by the works of the law, but by the faith of Jesus Christ, even we have believed in Jesus Christ, that we might be justified by the faith of Christ, and not by the works of the law: for by the works of the law shall no flesh be justified."

Ephesians 2:8–9: "For by grace are ye saved through faith; and that not of yourselves: it is the gift of God: Not of works, lest any man should boast."

"For they being ignorant of God's righteousness, and going about to establish their own righteousness, have not submitted themselves unto the righteousness of God." (Romans 10:3)

These passages underscore the principle that righteousness and salvation come through faith in Jesus Christ, not through adherence to the Law.

A Deeper Look into Law and Works vs. Faith and Grace

The parable of the rich man and Lazarus in Luke 16:19–31 is often seen as a stark portrayal of the consequences of ignoring the needy. However, when examined in the context of Christ's triumph and the overarching biblical narrative, it reveals a deeper message about the futility of seeking righteousness through the Law and the importance of faith and grace.

To further illustrate the spiritual torment of those who cling to the Law after Christ, Jesus gives a vivid parable—the story of the rich man and Lazarus. More than a moral tale, it uncovers the deep chasm between works and grace, legalism and faith, and points to the rest found only in Him.

The Parable Explained

Jesus tells the story of a rich man who lives in luxury while a beggar named Lazarus lies at his gate covered in sores and longing for crumbs from the rich man's table. When they both die, Lazarus is carried by angels to Abraham's bosom while the rich man finds himself in torment in Hades.

This parable is not just a moral lesson about charity but a profound commentary on the spiritual condition of Israel, especially its religious leaders who relied on the Law for righteousness.

Symbolism of the Rich Man and Lazarus

The Rich Man: Clothed in purple and fine linen, symbolizing wealth and high status, represents the religious elite of Israel who prided themselves on their adherence to the Law and their lineage from Abraham. His torment in Hades signifies the spiritual death and separation from God that comes from reliance on the Law without true faith.

Lazarus: A beggar covered in sores, representing the Gentiles or those marginalized by the religious system who seek mercy and crumbs of spiritual truth. Carried to Abraham's bosom, signifying the embrace of true faith and the inclusion of Gentiles into the promises of God through faith.

Jesus Himself hinted at this inclusion of the Gentiles into the covenantal blessings when He spoke with the Canaanite woman whose daughter was vexed by a devil. Initially, He answered her not a word. When pressed, He said, "I am not sent but unto the lost sheep of the house of Israel" (Matthew 15:24). Yet the woman persisted in faith, and Jesus responded with a striking statement:

"It is not meet to take the children's bread, and to cast it to dogs."

But she answered, "Truth, Lord: yet the dogs eat of the crumbs which fall from their masters' table." (v. 27)

Jesus marveled at her faith and granted her request. This moment prefigures the inclusion of Gentiles—those once considered outsiders—into the blessings of the kingdom. It reflects the same spiritual reality conveyed in the parable of Lazarus and the rich man, where Lazarus is comforted in Abraham's bosom.

Just as the faithful Gentile woman received what even many of the Jews rejected, so too the Gentiles, by faith, are grafted into the promises once given to Abraham.

In this parable, Lazarus represents those who refuse the mark—who hunger for righteousness through grace, not law.

The Great Gulf Fixed

The great gulf between Abraham and the rich man represents the insurmountable divide between those who seek justification by the Law and those who live by faith:

Galatians 3:10–11: "For as many as are of the works of the law are under the curse. The just shall live by faith."

Romans 1:17: "For therein is the righteousness of God revealed from faith to faith: as it is written, The just shall live by faith."

The Law, represented by Moses and the prophets, cannot bridge this gap; only faith in Christ can.

The Water of Life

The rich man's plea for a drop of water to cool his tongue underscores the torment of trying to achieve righteousness through works. Jesus, however, offers the water of life freely:

John 4:13–14: "Whosoever drinketh of this water shall thirst again: But whosoever drinketh of the water that I shall give him shall never thirst."

Revelation 21:6: "I will give unto him that is athirst of the fountain of the water of life freely."

This contrast highlights the spiritual satisfaction and rest found in grace compared to the endless striving under the Law.

The Role of Abraham

Abraham is central to this parable because he represents the promise of faith. The Jews took pride in their descent from Abraham, yet Jesus points out that true children of Abraham are those who follow his example of faith:

John 8:39: "If ye were Abraham's children, ye would do the works of Abraham."

Galatians 3:7: "Know ye therefore that they which are of faith, the same are the children of Abraham."

Abraham's bosom symbolizes the resting place of the faithful, those who trust in God's promises rather than their own works.

The False Hope of Works

The rich man's torment and his plea for Lazarus to warn his brothers illustrate the futility of relying on works for salvation. Abraham's response underscores that if they do not listen to Moses and the prophets—who all point to the necessity of faith—they will not be persuaded even by a resurrection:

Luke 16:29–31: "Abraham saith unto him, They have Moses and the prophets; let them hear them. If they hear not Moses and the prophets, neither will they be persuaded, though one rose from the dead."

The Jewish people had Moses and the prophets, not the Gentiles.

This parallels the rejection of Christ by many of the Jewish leaders despite His resurrection.

The Symbolism of 666: A Deeper Exploration

The number 666 mentioned in Revelation 13:18 is one of the most enigmatic and debated symbols in the Bible. Often associated with the "number of the beast," it carries profound symbolic meaning within the context of biblical numerology and the Jewish temple system. This section will delve into the deeper significance of 666, its connections to the Law, and its implications within the narrative of apostate Israel.

Revelation 13:18 provides the crucial passage: "Here is wisdom. Let him that hath understanding count the number of the beast: for it is the number of a man; and his number is Six hundred threescore and six." (Revelation 13:18)

This verse invites readers to discern the meaning behind the number 666, often interpreted as the epitome of human imperfection and rebellion against God.

Symbolism in the Jewish Temple System

The number 666 also has significant ties to the Jewish temple system and its practices. It can be viewed in the context of the dimensions and measurements of various temple structures and items, underscoring human elements within sacred rituals.

The Golden Image in Daniel 3: "Nebuchadnezzar the king made an image of gold, whose height was threescore cubits, and the breadth thereof six cubits." (Daniel 3:1) The image's dimensions (60x6 cubits) reflect human pride and idolatry. This physical image is made clearer now. Spiritual in Revelation with the new image signifying adherence to the law above divine authority.

Solomon's Gold: The scripture records the staggering amount of gold Solomon received annually: "Now the weight of gold that came to Solomon in one year was six hundred threescore and six talents of gold" (1 Kings 10:14). This very wealth enabled the lavish adornment of the temple, most significantly overlaying the entire Holy of Holies, or oracle, with pure gold (1 Kings 6:20). This provides a direct scriptural anchor, linking the number 666 to the peak of earthly power and the very materials consecrated for the holiest of purposes.

The High Priest and the Temple Service

The role of the high priest in the Jewish temple service is crucial in understanding the symbolism of 666. The high priest, representing humanity before God, performed rituals that highlighted the human element in seeking divine favor.

The high priest's duties and the temple's rituals, while ordained by God, were conducted by imperfect humans, symbolizing the inherent imperfection in the Law and the need for a perfect mediator, Jesus Christ.

Hebrews 7:23–28: "And they truly were many priests, because they were not suffered to continue by reason of death:

But this man, because he continueth ever, hath an unchangeable priesthood.

Wherefore he is able also to save them to the uttermost that come unto God by him, seeing he ever liveth to make intercession for them.

For such an high priest became us, who is holy, harmless, undefiled, separate from sinners, and made higher than the heavens;

Who needeth not daily, as those high priests, to offer up sacrifice, first for his own sins, and then for the people's: for this he did once, when he offered up himself.

For the law maketh men high priests which have infirmity; but the word of the oath, which was since the law, maketh the Son, who is consecrated for evermore."

The Wounded Head and the Illusion of Resurrection

One of the most mysterious images in Revelation 13 is this: "And I saw one of his heads as it were wounded to death; and his deadly wound was healed: and all the world wondered after the beast" (Revelation 13:3).

This is not merely a detail. It is the core of the beast's spiritual deception. Just as Christ was wounded and resurrected in glory, the beast mimics that victory with a false resurrection. But what exactly is the wounded head?

In the framework of Christ's timeline—unveiled earlier in Revelation 12—the wound is struck at Jesus' baptism. There, the heavens opened, and the true Son was revealed—not by temple rituals or priestly lineage, but by divine proclamation. When Jesus entered the wilderness and rejected Satan's temptations, the dragon's spiritual authority suffered a mortal blow. Legalism, performance-based righteousness, and institutional control were exposed as powerless against the Lamb.

This head—the one wounded—symbolizes the legal-religious system: the power of the law, the priesthood, and the temple structure that had ruled God's people. It was mortally wounded by Jesus' ministry. He forgave sins without sacrifice. He declared Himself greater than the temple. He overturned the tables of commerce and exposed the religious elite. He pronounced their system desolate.

But the wound was "healed." How? After His resurrection, the same system regained influence—not in truth, but in form. Legalism crept back, even among believers. The beast system revived, now clothed in religious garments once again. The healed head represents the resurgence of law-based religion—not as truth, but as a captivating counterfeit that draws back to performance, tradition, and control.

Just as the dragon wears crowns on his heads (spiritual power), the beast wears them on its horns (earthly control). The wounded and healed head is a chilling image: the resurrection of deception, not redemption. It is Satan's greatest illusion—a kingdom that looks alive, but leads to death.

The Beast and the Number of Man

Revelation 13 connects the number 666 with "the number of a man," emphasizing the human aspect of this symbolic beast. This represents humanity's flawed attempts to achieve righteousness and divine favor through their efforts rather than through faith in Christ, especially through the acts and works of the High Priest.

Just as 666 symbolizes imperfection, the Law reveals humanity's inability to achieve perfection through their works. This contrasts with the completeness and perfection found in Christ.

Number 600 – A Hidden Layer in 666

The number 600—the first digit of 666—symbolizes the totality of a special day, the Day of Atonement. To hold onto its works after Christ is to deny the true fulfillment of that rest. The 600 now becomes the shadow of what was holy—a symbol of man refusing to enter the rest offered by the Messiah.

To cling to the Law after Christ is to hold onto the shadow while rejecting the substance. The 600 thus becomes a symbol not of rest, but of refusal to rest in Christ's completed work—a rejection of the true Promised Land. This is a realized time, place, and person in an obsolete ritual of spiritual cleansing.

The Counterfeit Atonement: Decoding 666

The number of the beast is not a computer chip but a spiritual counterfeit. It is the number of a man-made system trying to do what only Christ could do. As Revelation 13:18 states, it is "the number of a man." It is a parody of holiness, an inverted Day of Atonement, structured in three layers of corruption:

6—The Number of Man (The Person): This represents the human High Priest. Though ordained, he was a flawed man who had to offer sacrifices for his own sin and whose work was never finished. It is the symbol of an insufficient priesthood that stands in contrast to Christ, our perfect High Priest.

60—The Corrupted Temple (The Place): This number symbolizes the sacred space—the Holy of Holies—that had become an idol in itself; a gilded shell where God's glory had departed.

The measurements of the Holy of Holies, the innermost and most sacred area of the Temple, are described in the Old Testament, particularly in the books of 1 Kings and 2 Chronicles in the context of Solomon's Temple, and in Ezekiel's vision of a future temple.

The key characteristic of the Holy of Holies in both descriptions is that it was a perfect cube. A cubit is an ancient unit of measurement, roughly equivalent to the length of a forearm, generally considered to be about 18 inches (45 centimeters).

In Solomon's Temple:

The dimensions are explicitly stated in 1 Kings 6:20:

"And the oracle in the forepart was twenty cubits in length, and twenty cubits in breadth, and twenty cubits in the height thereof: and he overlaid it with pure gold; and so covered the altar which was of cedar."

This is reiterated in 2 Chronicles 3:8:

"And he made the most holy house, the length whereof was according to the breadth of the house, twenty cubits, and the breadth thereof twenty cubits: and he overlaid it with fine gold, amounting to six hundred talents."

Thus, in Solomon's Temple, the Holy of Holies was a cube measuring:

Length: 20 cubits (approximately 30 feet or 9 meters)

Width: 20 cubits (approximately 30 feet or 9 meters)

Height: 20 cubits (approximately 30 feet or 9 meters)

In Ezekiel's Vision of the Temple:

The prophet Ezekiel was given a detailed vision of a future temple, and the dimensions of its Holy of Holies were consistent with those of Solomon's Temple, reinforcing the sacredness of this specific measurement.

Ezekiel 41:4:

"So he measured the length thereof, twenty cubits; and the breadth, twenty cubits, before the temple: and he said unto me, This is the most holy place."

In all these accounts, the perfect cubical shape of the Holy of Holies is thought to symbolize perfection, completeness, and the direct presence of God.

600—The Empty System (The Process): This represents the totality of the Old Covenant's legalistic system of sacrifices and rituals. It is the shadow clung to after the Substance, Christ, had come. It symbolizes a refusal to enter the true rest that Christ provides.

Together, 600, 60, and 6 form a false trinity of man's religious efforts: an empty system, a corrupted place, and a flawed person. It is the signature of a religion that has rejected its own fulfillment in Christ.

This understanding changes everything. The beast's number is no longer a mysterious code but a divine indictment—a counterfeit atonement that mimics the sacred, yet denies the Savior.

The beast's number is not merely sinister—it is a parody of holiness. It mimics sacred patterns of redemption but twists them into a lifeless system of control, guilt, and counterfeit sanctity. It is the embodiment of religion without Christ, atonement without blood, access without a veil torn.

In contrast, Jesus fulfilled every part of the true pattern:

He is the High Priest, not after the order of Aaron, but Melchizedek.

He entered the true tabernacle, not made with hands.

He offered His own blood, once for all.

And He secured eternal redemption (Hebrews 9:12).

The number of the beast is the number of a man—a man who tries to stand in the place of God, to offer a counterfeit priesthood, and to preserve a temple that Christ has already rendered obsolete.

Understanding 666 through the lens of the Day of Atonement unmasks the true deception, not merely political power or global tyranny, but the persistence of works-based religion masquerading as divine access.

The system Christ judged was not Rome or Caesar.

It was the temple system.

It was the priesthood.

It was the sacrifice that no longer saved.

And 666 stands as the signature of that entire fallen system—numbered, exposed, and judged by the Lamb.

Idolatry and Apostate Israel

The number 666 also symbolizes the spiritual idolatry and apostasy of Israel, who relied on the Law and their heritage for righteousness rather than faith in God.

Jeremiah 2:13: "For my people have committed two evils; they have forsaken me, the fountain of living waters, and hewed them out cisterns, broken cisterns, that can hold no water."

Ezekiel 16:15: "But thou didst trust in thine own beauty, and playedst the harlot because of thy renown, and pouredst out thy fornications on every one that passed by; his it was."

"Neither by the blood of goats and calves, but by his own blood he entered in once into the holy place, having obtained eternal redemption for us." (Hebrews 9:12)

—The deception is exposed. The beast has no dominion.

Seeing Beyond the Shadows: Rejecting the Idolatry of Objects

Just as the mark was not a physical symbol, but a spiritual allegiance, we must be cautious not to misplace holiness in physical form.

The deception of the beast system was not only legalistic—it was also external. It taught people to worship what could be seen, touched, and controlled. But true holiness has never been about visible form—it is about the presence of Christ within.

Even today, many fall into the same trap by attributing holiness to physical things: church buildings, religious symbols, crucifixes, or even the printed pages of a Bible. While the Word of God is eternal and sacred, the ink and paper are not. They can burn in a fire, but the truth they carry is spiritual and everlasting.

The New Covenant moved the focus from the external to the internal—from the shadow to the substance, which is Christ (Colossians 2:17).

As the writer of Hebrews explains, "For the law having a shadow of good things to come, and not the very image of the things, can never with those sacrifices which they offered year by year continually make the comers thereunto perfect" (Hebrews 10:1).

These rituals and visible forms were never the destination—they were signposts pointing to Christ. To return to them, or to treat any physical object as holy in itself, is to embrace the shadow while rejecting the light.

Paul writes with clarity:

"Wherefore if ye be dead with Christ from the rudiments of the world, why, as though living in the world, are ye subject to ordinances… (Touch not; taste not; handle not…) which all are to perish with the using?" (Colossians 2:21–22)

Jesus warned the woman at the well that worship would no longer be bound to any mountain or temple, but would be "in spirit and in truth" (John 4:23–24). No building is sacred unless the Spirit dwells within the people. No object carries divine power apart from the presence of God.

We must not mistake symbols for the substance they represent. The cross is not the power—the Lamb who died upon it is. The Bible is not holy because of its leather, paper, or ink—but because it points to the Living Word, Jesus Christ.

To bow before an object is to fall into the same deception as those who took the mark—trusting in what is visible, while missing the Spirit that gives life.

Let us see clearly, walk by the Spirit, and worship the One who dwells not in temples made with hands, but in the hearts of those made new.

Conclusion

The parable of the rich man and Lazarus profoundly illustrates the spiritual realities of law versus grace. It underscores that reliance on the Law and works leads to spiritual death and torment, while faith in Christ brings true rest and inclusion into the promises of God. This understanding aligns with the broader biblical narrative that emphasizes faith over works, grace over law, and the inclusivity of God's promises through faith in Jesus Christ.

The beast is legalism—salvation by works through the Law.

The false prophet is the high priest—enforcer of that system.

The image is the temple—a form of godliness denying the power.

The harlot is apostate Jerusalem—clinging to the Law and rejecting grace.

The number 666 is the works-based atonement—a false system, judged by the Lamb.

As Hebrews 10:1 declares, "For the law having a shadow of good things to come, and not the very image of the things..."—the entire beast system was a return to shadow. The true image is Christ. To receive His rest is to be sealed by the Spirit. To reject it is to receive the mark—not on the flesh, but on the hand of works and the forehead of mindful allegiance, where the old covenant once dwelled.

Let us not be deceived into religious performance—let us follow the Lamb and be marked by grace, not works; by trust, not fear. In every generation, legalism rises, but Christ has already conquered it. The true seal is the Spirit, and the true mark is love. In this knowledge, we live, and in this truth, we triumph.

Key Takeaways:

The Beast of Revelation 13 represents the spiritual system of legalism and apostate religion that stood in opposition to Christ's grace and truth, drawing from Daniel's typological power structures.

The "image of the beast" and its worship symbolize the Jerusalem Temple and its rituals after Christ's atoning work, representing a reliance on dead works rather than genuine faith.

The number 666 is the Old Covenant Day of Atonement, representing human efforts in religion without Christ (a flawed priesthood, corrupted temple, and empty system), in stark contrast to Christ's perfect and finished work.

Chapter 9

DIVINE WITNESSES: THE LAW AND THE PROPHETS

Divine Testimony

The testimony of law and prophecy in Revelation 11 invites profound exploration, like a tapestry woven from ancient wisdom and future promise.

As we embark on this journey, we must navigate the symbolic landscape where these witnesses embody the Law and the Prophets, serving as enduring spiritual principles rather than merely future physical entities.

Their story is not just a prophetic vision but a timeless reminder of the foundational truths that have guided humanity through millennia.

The Two Witnesses in Context

"And I will give power unto my two witnesses, and they shall prophesy a thousand two hundred and threescore days, clothed in sackcloth. These are the two olive trees, and the two candlesticks standing before the God of the earth." (Revelation 11:3–4)

But what do these witnesses represent? And how do they fit into God's redemptive story?

These verses invite us into a mysterious yet familiar realm where the identities of the witnesses are not explicitly disclosed.

Are they Moses and Elijah, or perhaps Moses and Enoch? While some interpretations suggest a literal return of these figures, this chapter advocates for a more symbolic understanding.

The witnesses are seen not as future individuals but as representations of the Law and the Prophets, testifying to their enduring spiritual truths.

Moses and Elijah: The Law and the Prophets

To fully grasp the significance of the dual testimony of law and prophecy, we must first delve into the historical and spiritual roles of Moses and Elijah.

Moses, the central lawgiver of the Old Testament, received the divine Law on Mount Sinai.

His leadership of the Israelites and his fervent commitment to God's commands have cemented his place as the quintessential lawgiver.

Elijah, on the other hand, stands as a beacon of prophetic zeal.

Known for his passionate defense of the true faith amidst rampant idolatry, Elijah's confrontations with false prophets on Mount Carmel vividly illustrate the consequences of straying from divine truth.

The requirement for "two or three witnesses" in Old Testament legal matters (Deuteronomy 17:6) underscores the importance of corroborated testimony. In the context of Revelation, this legal principle takes on a profound spiritual dimension, highlighting the weight of the combined testimony of the Law and the Prophets.

Symbolic Actions and Their Significance

In Revelation 11:5–6, the actions of the witnesses echo those of Moses and Elijah in the Old Testament, further cementing their symbolic connection to the Law and the Prophets.

Moses and Elijah, whose miracles included turning water to blood and fire from heaven, exemplify the divine authority vested in these witnesses.

This parallelism reinforces the idea that their presence in Revelation is not about predicting their physical return but about affirming the enduring significance of their spiritual message.

Throughout the Old Testament, the Law and the Prophets stood as witnesses to the idolatry, apostasy, and blasphemy in Jerusalem. Their warnings and exhortations were aimed at guiding the people back to righteousness. This same role is envisioned for the witnesses in Revelation, where they symbolize a call to repentance and spiritual renewal in the face of moral decline.

Sackcloth and Repentance

The imagery of the witnesses "covered in prophetic mourning" (Revelation 11:3) evokes a powerful symbol of mourning and repentance. In the Old Testament, sackcloth was worn as an expression of contrition and sorrow for sins. In Revelation, this attire signifies the urgent need for repentance in Jerusalem's spiritual decline. The witnesses, embodying the Law and the Prophets, serve as a stark reminder of the consequences of turning away from God's commands.

Persecution and Triumph

The narrative of the dual testimony of law and prophecy in Revelation 11:7–10 describes their persecution and eventual martyrdom, mirroring the fates of many prophets throughout biblical history. This persecution highlights the resistance to God's message and its consequences. However, their ultimate vindication in Revelation 11:11–12, where they are resurrected and ascend to heaven, symbolizes the triumph of God's truth and the enduring power of the Law and the Prophets.

Reflecting on the dual testimony of law and prophecy reminds us of the crucial role that the Law and the Prophets have played in guiding God's people throughout history. Their message remains a source of guidance, warning, and hope. The witnesses in Revelation symbolize this enduring message, emphasizing the vital role of God's Word in shaping human history. They call us to a deeper understanding of repentance, justice, and faithfulness, echoing through the ages and culminating in the person of Jesus Christ.

Today, just as the Law and the Prophets bore witness to the truth in their time, we are called to be living witnesses of Christ's fulfillment. Their prophetic voice now echoes through us—urging our generation to repentance, justice, and unwavering faith. To embody their testimony is to walk in Christ's light and truth—shining faithfully in a world that still resists it.

The Transfiguration: A Symbolic Affirmation

In the intricate landscape of biblical interpretation, the Transfiguration stands as a luminous tableau that some invoke as evidence for the literal return of Moses and Elijah as the dual testimony of law and prophecy in Revelation.

The dazzling scene on the mountaintop, where Jesus is transfigured before Peter, James, and John, unfolds with Moses and Elijah appearing alongside the glorified Christ.

This celestial encounter, however, does not herald a future physical return of Moses and Elijah.

Instead, it serves as a profound affirmation of Christ's fulfillment of the Law and the Prophets.

The brilliance of the Transfiguration lies in its symbolic resonance, transcending the confines of literalism.

Prophetic Continuity and Divine Plan

A pivotal moment supporting this understanding emerges in the concluding verses of the Old Testament book of Malachi. Malachi 4:5–6 prophetically declares:

"Behold, I will send you Elijah the prophet before the coming of the great and dreadful day of the Lord:

And he shall turn the heart of the fathers to the children, and the heart of the children to their fathers, lest I come and smite the earth with a curse."

This Old Testament anticipation finds its echo in the New Testament, specifically in the Gospel of Luke 1:17, as the angel Gabriel announces the birth of John the Baptist to Zechariah:

"And he shall go before him in the spirit and power of Elias, to turn the hearts of the fathers to the children, and the disobedient to the wisdom of the just; to make ready a people prepared for the Lord."

The seamless connection between the Old and New Testaments resonates with divine continuity.

John the Baptist, embodying the spirit and power of Elijah, becomes the herald of the Messiah, bridging the prophetic legacy of the Old Testament with its fulfillment in the New.

Therefore, when we encounter the Transfiguration scene with Moses and Elijah standing beside the transfigured Christ, it beckons us to embrace a symbolic reading.

Moses represents the Law, and Elijah, the quintessential prophet, encapsulates the prophetic tradition.

Together, they testify that God's promises are fulfilled in Jesus Christ.

The Law and the Prophets Fulfilled in Christ

The 1,260 days of the two witnesses—often viewed as literal future time—are better understood as symbolic of the prophetic era culminating in Christ. The two witnesses, Moses and Elijah, represent the Law and the Prophets, and Jesus did not just follow them—He fulfilled them.

As He declared, "Think not that I am come to destroy the law, or the prophets: I am not come to destroy, but to fulfil" (Matthew 5:17). These two witnesses "prophesy" until Christ appears—the Light to which their testimony pointed. Their witness corresponds not to a future event, but to the ministry of Jesus Himself, who fulfills their voice, embodies their message, and brings their partial witness to completion.

Jesus confirmed this when He said, "The law and the prophets were until John: since that time the kingdom of God is preached, and every man presseth into it" (Luke 16:16). This declaration marks a spiritual shift: the Law and the Prophets had fulfilled their witness. Likewise, Paul wrote, "But now the righteousness of God without the law is manifested, being witnessed by the law and the prophets" (Romans 3:21). These witnesses were never the destination, but the signposts that testified of the Messiah. In Revelation 11, their symbolic ministry concludes not in defeat but in fulfillment—as their testimony is completed, and the gospel of the kingdom emerges in power.

In this light, the "death" of the witnesses reflects the silencing of the Old Covenant. Their "resurrection" represents not only their vindication but their transformation—raised not as returning individuals, but as fulfilled voices now living within the gospel of Christ. The spiritual truth they proclaimed now lives on in every believer who carries forward their testimony.

Conclusion: The True Witness

In this exploration, the layers of Scripture unfold, revealing deep truths that go far beyond a surface reading.

The prophetic voices, echoing from Malachi to Luke, harmonize to unveil the rich convergence of symbolism and substance in a sacred dance across the pages of Scripture.

The emergence of the dual testimony of law and prophecy in Revelation 11 is a powerful testament to the enduring relevance of the Law and the Prophets.

Through their symbolic presence, we are reminded of the crucial role of these spiritual principles in guiding humanity.

The narrative invites us to see beyond a literal interpretation and embrace a deeper understanding of the witnesses as eternal bearers of divine truth.

We are not spectators of future terror—we are citizens of present glory.

From Moses and Elijah to John the Baptist and Revelation's visions, their story reveals a divine continuity that transcends time. This unified testimony calls us to heed the timeless message of repentance, justice, and faithfulness, echoing through the ages and culminating in the person of Jesus Christ.

Their witness, now ours, lives on—calling us to stand, speak, and shine.

Key Takeaways:

The "Two Witnesses" in Revelation 11 symbolize the enduring spiritual principles of the Law and the Prophets, not literal future individuals.

Their testimony, martyrdom, and resurrection signify the culmination and vindication of the Old Covenant's message in Christ, whose ministry fulfilled all that the Law and Prophets foretold.

The Transfiguration scene (Moses and Elijah with Christ) further affirms Jesus as the fulfillment of both the Law and the Prophets, demonstrating that John the Baptist, in the spirit of Elijah, prepared the way for the Messiah.

The resurrection and ascension of the witnesses symbolize the transformation and glorification of the Old Covenant within the New—where the Law and the Prophets are no longer external codes or distant voices, but internalized in Christ and alive in His people.

Chapter 10

REVELATION'S TIMELINE : CHRIST'S MINISTRY

Rediscovering the True Timeline

Beneath Revelation's layers of symbols lies something far greater: the complete, spiritual vison of Jesus Christ's redemptive work, perfectly mirrored through its visions. Revelation is not about what will happen, but what has happened—through Christ's life, ministry, death, resurrection, ascension, the outpouring of the Spirit, and His ongoing reign through His people.

When we follow the divine chronology woven into Revelation, we find ourselves walking the very path of Jesus' redemptive journey—from the final cries of the Law and the Prophets, through His public revealing, the spiritual war He waged, the authority He claimed, the Spirit He poured out, and the kingdom He established. This is the true timeline Revelation reveals—a story of victory, fulfillment, and the everlasting reign of Christ, now made manifest in us.

Revelation 5 – Resurrection and the Unsealing of Redemption

The spiritual sequence of spiritual victory opens in the majestic throne room of heaven, where a scroll rests in the right hand of the One seated upon the throne. This scroll, sealed with seven seals, holds the divine mysteries of God's redemptive plan—veiled from creation and awaiting their appointed revealing.

A mighty angel cries out, "Who is worthy to open the scroll and to loose its seals?" But no one in heaven, on earth, or under the earth is found worthy. A heavy silence descends upon heaven—a silence that mirrors the ache of centuries. John begins to weep bitterly, overcome with grief at the thought that God's redemptive plan might remain forever sealed.

This sorrow is not merely John's; it is the echo of a nation and a world groaning under the weight of unfulfilled promise. For four hundred years—from the final words of Malachi to the cry of John the Baptist in the wilderness—heaven had been silent. The scroll of the Old Covenant stood complete, yet unopened, like a legal document awaiting its fulfillment.

But then, a voice pierces the silence. One of the elders says, "Weep not: behold, the Lion of the tribe of Judah, the Root of David, hath prevailed to open the book." (Revelation 5:5)

John turns to behold this conquering Lion—but what he sees is shocking.

He sees not a lion, but a Lamb, standing as though it had been slain. The marks of crucifixion are still upon Him, yet He stands alive—resurrected and glorified. This is no contradiction. It is the mystery revealed: the Lion conquers by becoming the Lamb. Through suffering, He has overcome. Through death, He has brought life.

The scroll is not merely a vision—it is the Revelation itself. Just as Revelation 1:1 declares, "The Revelation of Jesus Christ, which God gave unto Him," so now, in Revelation 5, we see that divine transfer unfold. The Father gives the Revelation to the Son, and the Son gives it to His servants.

Through His resurrection, Jesus does more than conquer death—He unlocks the hidden mysteries of God's eternal plan. What was once sealed is now revealed.

The Heavenly Door Opens: Resurrection, Ascension, and Revelation 4–5

To fully grasp the chronology unfolding in Revelation, it is crucial to align the heavenly scenes of Revelation 4 and 5 with the resurrection and ascension of Jesus. Revelation 4 begins with a striking statement:

"After this I looked, and, behold, a door was opened in heaven: and the first voice which I heard was as it were of a trumpet talking with me; which said, Come up hither, and I will shew thee things which must be hereafter." (Revelation 4:1)

Up to this point, John had been witnessing earthly scenes—the letters to the seven churches. But now, he is transported through an opened door into the heavenly dimension. This transition is not arbitrary; it marks a decisive shift—from earth to heaven, from the Old Covenant's warnings to the New Covenant's inauguration through Christ.

This moment in the heavenly courts corresponds with Christ's resurrection and ascension. Revelation 4:1, where John goes through the door in heaven, is the very ascension of Christ to heaven after the resurrection. John describes the throne and then Jesus is handed the sealed scroll and is declared worthy to receive all power, all authority, and the fullness of God's redemptive Revelation. As He approaches the throne and takes the scroll from the hand of the Father, heaven erupts in worship. The Lamb has triumphed. He alone is worthy to open what was sealed.

When Mary Magdalene first encounters the risen Jesus, He says:

"Touch me not; for I am not yet ascended to my Father..." (John 20:1)

Shortly thereafter, Jesus appears to His disciples, invites them to touch Him (Luke 24:39), and even eats before them (Luke 24:41–43), demonstrating that He has since ascended and returned. What happened in between?

It is in this unseen moment between the tomb and the upper room that we find the heavenly drama of Revelation 4–5 unfolding. Jesus ascended to the Father, presented Himself as the Lamb that was slain, and was declared worthy to receive the sealed scroll—the Revelation itself.

This heavenly enthronement matches His triumphant declaration in Matthew 28:18:

"All power is given unto me in heaven and in earth."

The reason Jesus could now say "all power" had been given was that He had just been to the Father. His victory at the cross was validated by the Father, and His authority was publicly declared in heaven and on earth.

The song sung in Revelation 5 confirms this transition from Old to New:

"And they sung a new song, saying, Thou art worthy to take the book, and to open the seals thereof: for Thou wast slain, and hast redeemed us to God by Thy blood out of every kindred, and tongue, and people, and nation;

And hast made us unto our God kings and priests: and we shall reign on the earth. (Revelation 5:9–10)

This "new song" contrasts the "song of Moses" (Exodus 15:1)—the old deliverance song after Egypt—with a new and greater deliverance through the Lamb. The Lamb's ascension and coronation in the throne room of heaven fulfill the spiritual climax of redemption.

Thus, Revelation 4 and 5 are not abstract visions of a distant future. They are the heavenly emergence of what occurred immediately after the resurrection. The opened door, the Lamb before the throne, and the worship of heaven all mark the inauguration of Christ's reign and the beginning of the unfolding Revelation.

The redemptive story written before the foundation of the world now unfolds, not as a future catastrophe, but as a victorious kingdom already set in motion through Christ.

This spiritual timeline does not begin with fear, judgment, or end-time terror. It begins with worship. It begins with victory. It begins with a slain Lamb who stands—alive, triumphant, and enthroned—ready to unveil the spiritual Kingdom of God made manifest in the hearts of His people.

The Victorious Return: Revelation 19 and the Disciples

Just as Revelation 5 unveils heaven's response to Christ's resurrection, Revelation 19 symbolically unveils His victorious return to His disciples. Many have read this passage as a distant future event, but viewed through a spiritual lens, it aligns powerfully with Jesus' first post-resurrection appearance.

He returns robed in glory, crowned with many crowns, His name exalted above all names—just as He declared to His disciples, "All power is given unto me in heaven and in earth" (Matthew 28:18). The white horse He rides represents spiritual authority; the armies that follow reflect the host of heaven bearing witness to His triumph.

The "marriage supper of the Lamb" is not postponed to some far-off feast—it begins in the Upper Room, as the Bridegroom reunites with His Bride, breathes His Spirit upon them (John 20:22), and prepares them to carry His Kingdom to the nations. This is the coronation moment manifest on earth: the return of the risen King to those He loves.

Rather than seeing Revelation 19 as disconnected from Christ's resurrection, this perspective harmonizes it with His reappearance to the very ones who had watched Him suffer, die, and now stand in awe of His risen glory.

Revelation 6–7 – The Seals and the Decline of the Old Order

As the Lamb begins to open the seals, what unfolds is not a prophecy of global disaster but a spiritual revelation of the world Jesus stepped into—the final breaths of the Old Covenant age. These seals expose the decayed condition of Israel and humanity at large, still bound under law, weighed down by sin, and spiritually blind to the arrival of their Messiah.

Each seal reveals a symptom of a world ruled by legalism and religious pride. The white horse represents false messianic hopes. The red horse echoes the violence and spiritual unrest of a nation ready to revolt. The black horse mirrors prophetic famine. And the pale horse brings death, the inevitable result of a system that cannot give life. These are not literal events but spiritual realities that defined the world of Old Covenant Israel.

This is the stage upon which the Messiah would soon step—an Israel groaning under Roman oppression, corrupted priesthood, and empty religious ritual. The Law had revealed the sickness, but could not provide the cure. The prophets had warned of judgment, but their voices were fading. The hearts of the people were hardened, and the hope of redemption had become buried beneath centuries of disappointment.

Yet amidst this spiritual ruin, Revelation 7 offers a pause—a glimpse of divine mercy. A remnant is sealed. These are not literal numbers but symbolic of a preserved people, those who would recognize the Lamb and receive the Spirit. It is a vision of preservation in the midst of judgment. The sealing does not exempt them from suffering, but marks them for salvation.

This moment marks the last cries of an old world passing away. The Old Covenant had served its purpose, and now, through the Lamb, a new age was dawning. The seals reveal not the end of the world, but the end of an age—the legalistic system of the Old Covenant crumbling under the weight of its own inability to save.

Revelation 11 – The Two Witnesses: The Law and the Prophets Complete Their Testimony

Before Christ is publicly revealed in His ministry, the voices of the Old Covenant still echo through the land. Revelation 11 introduces the Two Witnesses, mysterious figures standing with divine authority. But they are not two future individuals arriving at the end of history—they are symbols of something far more ancient and foundational: the Law and the Prophets.

This symbolic pair had long testified to God's righteousness. Moses, the giver of the Law, and Elijah, the fiery prophet who called Israel to repentance, serve as archetypes of these two enduring witnesses. Together, they stood as the spiritual backbone of Israel's covenant identity—constantly calling God's people back to faithfulness.

Revelation portrays them covered in prophetic mourning, echoing their long-standing call to repentance and mourning over sin. Their testimony spans "a thousand two hundred and threescore days," symbolizing the completeness of their prophetic mission. Yet even as they speak, the world resists. The beast rises, and the witnesses are slain—symbolizing the rejection and apparent silencing of the Old Covenant's authority.

But death is not the end of their story. After three and a half days, the Spirit of life from God enters them, and they stand upon their feet. This resurrection is not about a literal return—it is about vindication. What the Law and the Prophets declared has been fulfilled in Christ. Their testimony is validated, their voices glorified.

Jesus confirms this transition when He declares, "The law and the prophets were until John" (Luke 16:16). With the arrival of John the Baptist—the final prophet crying in the wilderness—the age of prophetic foretelling reaches its crescendo. The Old Covenant has said all it can say. The witnesses have completed their testimony.

Their symbolic death marks the end of an era; their symbolic resurrection points to Christ as the fulfillment of their every word. The torch has been passed. The Law and the Prophets now find their full expression in Him, and the redemptive timeline presses forward with new clarity.

Revelation 8–11 – The Trumpets: Prophetic Warnings Before the Baptism

As we move further along the spiritual timeline, the Trumpets of Revelation sound not as instruments of chaos, but as clarion calls of urgency—last warnings before the Messiah is publicly revealed. These trumpet blasts are symbolic of the final prophetic cries, a series of escalating spiritual alarms announcing the soon arrival of the Kingdom of God.

Throughout Scripture, trumpets are used to signal divine activity. They announce God's presence at Sinai. They call the people to repentance. They rally the faithful for spiritual battle. In this context, the trumpets of Revelation mirror the final cries of the prophets, especially the voice of John the Baptist: "Prepare ye the way of the Lord!"

Each trumpet intensifies the call. They are not literal catastrophes, but vivid symbolic messages of judgment upon hardened hearts and corrupt systems. These visions reveal the spiritual consequences of rejecting God's messengers—the erosion of truth, the decay of righteousness, the spiritual blindness that darkens the land. The Old Covenant's warnings are reaching their climax, and time is running out.

In the final trumpet, the seventh, we hear a declaration: "The kingdoms of this world are become the kingdoms of our Lord, and of his Christ" (Revelation 11:15). This is not the beginning of future chaos—it is the announcement that the King has come. The baptism of Jesus is imminent. The heavens are about to open, the Spirit will descend, and the Father will declare His Son to the world.

Thus, the trumpets lead us to the threshold of a new covenant reality. They mark the final sounds of the old order before the Messiah emerges. In this spiritual chronology, the trumpets are the last cries of the Law and Prophets—echoes calling for repentance—before the Lamb steps forward to begin His public ministry.

Revelation 12 – The Baptism and the Beginning of Ministry

Revelation 12 unveils one of the most vivid and spiritually symbolic scenes in the entire book. A woman clothed with the sun cries out in travail, about to give birth. A great red dragon stands ready to devour her child as soon as it is born. But the child is caught up to God and to His throne, and the woman flees into the wilderness where she is protected.

This is no apocalyptic fantasy—it is a symbolic retelling of Christ's baptism and the beginning of His earthly ministry.

The woman represents faithful Israel, the remnant through whom the Messiah comes forth. The male child is Jesus, born not only in the flesh but now publicly revealed at His baptism. This is the moment the heavens open, the Spirit descends like a dove, and the Father proclaims, "This is my beloved Son, in whom I am well pleased." It is the spiritual birth of the kingdom, the divine vision of the King.

The dragon—identified as Satan—stands ready to oppose this redemptive plan. No longer content to corrupt through deceit, he now seeks open confrontation. As Jesus is baptized and led into the wilderness, the spiritual war ignites. Satan tempts Him, challenges His identity, and tries to thwart His mission. But Jesus prevails.

"I saw Satan fall like lightning from heaven," Jesus later declares (Luke 10:18). Revelation 12 presents this same truth in visionary form: the dragon is cast out of heaven, no longer able to accuse the brethren. He has defeated the enemy and launched His ministry with authority.

The woman fleeing into the wilderness mirrors the faithful remnant—those who would later follow Christ, endure tribulation, and be preserved by God. The wilderness is not abandonment; it is divine protection. It is where the new people of God are nourished, even as war rages in the unseen realms.

This is the true meaning of Revelation 12: the baptism of Jesus, the launching of His ministry, the beginning of the spiritual war, and the clear declaration that the invisible Kingdom of God is now at hand. The timeline continues, and the Lamb now walks among us—teaching, healing, confronting, and building a kingdom not made with hands.

Revelation 15–16 – The Bowls of Wrath: Spiritual Outpourings During Ministry

As Jesus moves through His earthly ministry, Revelation 15 and 16 symbolically portray what are often misunderstood as catastrophic end-time judgments. In truth, these "bowls of wrath" are already realized plagues—they are the spiritual outpourings of Christ's ministry itself on Jerusalem and upon His entrance. These are the moments in which divine truth confronts human rebellion, where mercy challenges hardness of heart, and where light exposes darkness.

Each bowl represents a direct spiritual action taken by Jesus against the old systems of sin, legalism, and religious hypocrisy. These are not literal disasters—they are acts of purification. They are the moments when Jesus heals the sick on the Sabbath, confronts the corruption of temple commerce, calls out the self-righteousness of the Pharisees, and offers grace to the outcast. In each of these acts, He pours out divine truth that challenges and dismantles the foundations of the old order.

To the unrepentant heart, grace feels like judgment. To those who clung to power and pride, Christ's love was unbearable. One bowl is poured upon the seat of the beast—symbolizing the authority of the religious system— and it brings darkness. Not because God sends chaos, but because the light of truth exposes deception. The judgment is inherent in the confrontation.

Jesus confirms this spiritual interpretation when He declares, "Now is the judgment of this world: now shall the prince of this world be cast out" (John 12:31). The true wrath of God is not rage—it is righteous confrontation. It is the clarity that breaks through lies. It is the presence of the Lamb walking in power, truth, and compassion, dismantling every false stronghold.

Revelation 16's bowls are the invisible, yet powerful, proclamations of Jesus' ministry in Jerusalem. They represent the disruptive force of divine love confronting institutional sin. They are the spiritual consequences of rejecting the Messiah even as He walks in their midst. And they are the final cracks in the walls of the old world—preparing the way for a kingdom not built on law, but on grace and truth.

Revelation 19 – The Resurrection and Declaration of Authority

Following His crucifixion, Jesus rises in glory. The tomb is empty, death is defeated, and the Lamb who was slain now stands as the triumphant King. Revelation 19 captures this victory—not as a future battle yet to be fought, but as a present reality inaugurated in the resurrection.

Heaven opens, and Christ rides forth on a white horse, crowned with many crowns, and called Faithful and True. This dramatic image is not of a war to come, but of a conquest achieved. It is the divine proclamation that Jesus, having conquered sin and death, now rules with all authority in heaven and on earth.

This moment corresponds with the Great Commission, where the risen Christ appears to His disciples and declares, "All power is given unto me in heaven and in earth" (Matthew 28:18). The King is enthroned. The Lamb is exalted. The kingdom has come—not in military might or political force, but in the resurrection of the Son of God.

The Redeemed in Triumph: Heaven's Procession on Earth

The "armies of heaven" that follow Him are not angels descending for battle, but the company of the redeemed—clothed in fine linen, which is the righteousness of the saints. They are the saints, now empowered to carry forth His reign on earth. Their weapon is not a sword of steel, but the sharp word of truth proceeding from the mouth of the King.

Revelation 19's language of judgment and conquest is symbolic of the triumph of Christ's finished work. The beast and false prophet—representing corrupt religious and political systems—are cast down, because their power has been broken at the cross. The Word of God has prevailed. The Lamb has overcome.

This vision is not a preview, it is a coronation. It reveals the spiritual authority of Christ following His resurrection. The King rides forth, not to wage war, but to proclaim His victory and to establish His rule through His people. The reign of Christ is not something we await—it is something we now live in, because the resurrection is not just a moment in time—it is the eternal turning point of all creation.

Revelation 20 – Pentecost and the Reign of the Saints

From Christ's resurrection flows the next pivotal moment in redemptive history—Pentecost. Revelation 20, often interpreted as a distant, mysterious millennium, is actually a vivid spiritual portrayal of what took place when the Holy Spirit was poured out and the Church was born.

This chapter opens with the binding of Satan, symbolizing the restriction of his deceptive power. No longer can he blind the nations as he once did. With the resurrection and ascension of Christ, and the coming of the Holy Spirit, the strong man is bound so that his house may be plundered. The gospel goes forth freely. Light shines into darkness. The truth begins to spread to every nation, tribe, and tongue.

Pentecost marks the first resurrection—a spiritual awakening. Those who were dead in sin are made alive in Christ. The saints reign, not from political thrones, but as a royal priesthood in the Kingdom of God. As Revelation says, "They lived and reigned with Christ a thousand years." This is symbolic of the fullness and completeness of the Church age—a perfect span, divinely appointed.

Those who partake in this first resurrection—the born-again believers empowered by the Spirit—are no longer under the power of the second death. They are sealed, sanctified, and commissioned. The Church becomes His body, His temple, His city.

This reign is not a utopia, nor is it without opposition. But it is real, present, and powerful. Christ reigns through the lives of those who love Him, and the Spirit empowers them to overcome evil with good. Revelation 20 is not waiting to be fulfilled—it is already fulfilled at Pentecost. The saints are seated with Christ in heavenly places. The kingdom is alive and advancing.

This is the age in which we live—the age of the Spirit, the age of the reigning saints, the age of the Gospel's unstoppable power.

Revelation 21–22 – The New Jerusalem: The Kingdom Now

The redemptive timeline reaches its glorious climax in the final chapters of Revelation—not with the destruction of the earth, but with the debut of the New Jerusalem. This is not a city descending from the sky in some future age—it is the present, spiritual manifestation of the Church, the Bride of Christ, revealed in all her glory.

This is not describing heaven—it is describing the indwelling Kingdom of God made manifest through Christ.

The city has no temple, for the Lord God Almighty and the Lamb are its temple.

It needs no sun or moon, for the glory of God lights it.

The river of life flows from the throne, and the tree of life bears fruit for the healing of the nations.

183

These are not physical attributes—they are spiritual realities.

It is the Church radiant with grace, empowered by the Spirit, and rooted in the eternal presence of Christ.

Paul affirms this in Galatians when he says, "But Jerusalem which is above is free, which is the mother of us all." Hebrews tells us we have already "come unto Mount Sion, and unto the city of the living God, the heavenly Jerusalem." We are not waiting for this city—it has already come. We are its citizens.

The message of Revelation ends not with anxiety, but with invitation. "The Spirit and the bride say, Come." It is a call to enter what has already been established. The gates are never shut. The river never stops flowing. The Lamb is always present. This is the kingdom that cannot be shaken—the New Jerusalem that shines with eternal light.

This is the end of the timeline and the beginning of life. The story has been fulfilled. The Revelation has been unveiled.

Key Takeaways:

Revelation unveils a spiritual timeline reflecting Christ's redemptive work, from His resurrection and ascension (Rev 4-5) to the outpouring of the Spirit (Rev 20) and the establishment of His ongoing reign (Rev 21-22).

The breaking of the Seals (Rev 6-7) reveals the decline and spiritual condition of the Old Covenant age, while the Trumpets (Rev 8-11) signify prophetic warnings before Christ's public ministry.

The Bowls of Wrath (Rev 15-16) represent the spiritual outpourings of Christ's ministry upon entering Jerusalem, confronting legalism and hypocrisy, culminating in His crucifixion and the irreversible shaking of the old system.

The Spiritual Timeline of Revelation and the Life of Christ

Revelation Chapter	Vision or Event	Spiritual Fulfillment in Christ's Life/Ministry
Rev 1	John sees Jesus among the lampstands	High Priestly appearance to John
Rev 2-3	Letters to the seven churches	Jesus' warning and correction to His body
Rev 4	Heavenly throne revealed	Jesus' ascension into heaven (After Resurrection)
Rev 5	Lamb takes the scroll	Jesus receives all power after resurrection (Matt. 28:18)
Rev 6	Seals opened	Prophetic revelation of judgments (Prior to Christ)
Rev 7	Sealing of spiritual Israel	Gentiles and Jews spiritually sealed; inclusive new covenant
Rev 8-9	Trumpet judgments	Ministry of John the Baptist
Rev 10	Angel with the little book	The new covenant message

Revelation Chapter	Vision or Event	Spiritual Fulfillment in Christ's Life/Ministry
Rev 11	Two witnesses & temple measured	Law and prophets testify; spiritual Jerusalem's condition assessed
Rev 12	Woman, child, and dragon	Jesus' baptism; Satan's fall; spiritual warfare
Rev 13	Beast and false prophet rise	Legalism, the Law, and religious oppression
Rev 14	Lamb on Mt. Zion; harvest	Faithful followers redeemed; Jesus as firstfruits of resurrection
Rev 15-16	Bowls of wrath poured	Jesus bears the full wrath (crucifixion); Jerusalem and their Messiah
Rev 17	Harlot revealed	Apostate Jerusalem exposed
Rev 18	Harlot judged and falls	Jerusalem condemned for rejecting Christ
Rev 19	Rider on white horse appears	Jesus' post-resurrection appearances to the disciples and others
Rev 20	Satan bound, judgment begins	Pentecost, Spirit poured out, new covenant kingdom empowered

Revelation Chapter	Vision or Event	Spiritual Fulfillment in Christ's Life/Ministry
Rev 21	New heaven and new earth	Church as the New Jerusalem, God's dwelling with man, The Kingdom of God
Rev 22	River of life and eternal communion	Eternal life flowing from Christ; the Spirit's ongoing work

Chapter 11

THE RIDER AND THE WINEPRESS: THE KING OF KINGS

The Vision of Victory

Revelation 19 does not present a future battlefield, but a present throne room.

It is not a forecast of impending war, but the declaration of a completed triumph.

In its vivid imagery of heaven opening and a rider on a white horse emerging, we are not invited to anticipate a coming battle, but to behold a King who has already conquered.

This chapter unveils the spiritual coronation of Jesus Christ following His resurrection, proclaiming Him as the reigning and triumphant King of kings and Lord of lords, then His return to earth to appear to His disciples.

The resurrection of Jesus is not merely a historical event; it is the eternal turning point of all creation. It marks the defeat of death, the silencing of the accuser, and the exaltation of the Lamb. In Revelation 19, the heavens respond to this triumph with worship, as the multitude in heaven shouts, "Alleluia; Salvation, and glory, and honour, and power, unto the Lord our God" (Revelation 19:1).

The Triumphant King Unveiled: The Exalted Christ

"And I saw heaven opened, and behold a white horse; and he that sat upon him was called Faithful and True, and in righteousness he doth judge and make war".

This moment is not about a future war; it is about the authority and reign that Christ has already received. The Rider is the risen Christ, not as the suffering Servant, but as the enthroned King. The white horse symbolizes victory, and the One who rides upon it is not preparing for conquest—He is returning from it.

His name, "Faithful and True," reflects His perfect obedience and covenant fulfillment. His eyes are as a flame of fire, penetrating all pretense, and on His head are many crowns, signifying the fullness of His dominion. These crowns are not given in anticipation, but in recognition. He is crowned because He has overcome. He speaks as the risen Christ who returned to His disciples, not as a conqueror with a sword in His hand, but as the Conqueror with the Word in His mouth.

"And he was clothed with a vesture dipped in blood: and his name is called The Word of God". This echoes the prophet Isaiah, who saw a triumphant figure with red apparel after treading the winepress alone (Isaiah 63:1-3). The red-stained garments reflect the judgment upon apostate Jerusalem. The winepress He has trodden represents the spiritual judgment on a covenant-breaking people—those who rejected the Messiah and crucified the Lord of glory. The blood is not His own but theirs. The imagery points to the crushing of rebellion, the wrath poured out upon the unfaithful city, and the vindication of the righteous.

The weapon of this King is not of this world. "And out of his mouth goeth a sharp sword…". This two-edged sword is not steel—it is Scripture. As Hebrews 4:12 says, "For the word of God is quick, and powerful, and sharper than any twoedged sword". This is not violence; it is victory by truth. Christ conquers not by bloodshed, but by revelation.

Following Him are the armies of heaven, clothed in fine linen, white and clean. These are not angels descending with weapons; they are the redeemed. Their white robes are their righteousness, made clean by the blood of the Lamb, and they share in His triumph. Their power is in their testimony, for "they overcame him by the blood of the Lamb, and by the word of their testimony".

Finally, the beast and the false prophet are cast into the lake of fire. This is not a future drama, but the reality that Christ's resurrection disarmed all competing rulers and authorities. As Colossians 2:15 declares: "And having spoiled principalities and powers, he made a shew of them openly, triumphing over them in it". Their power was broken at the cross, and their deception is unmasked by the gospel.

The Garment Dipped in Blood: The Fulfillment of Isaiah 63

John writes, "And he was clothed with a vesture dipped in blood: and his name is called The Word of God" (Revelation 19:13). This verse directly parallels the haunting and powerful imagery of Isaiah 63:

"Who is this that cometh from Edom, with dyed garments from Bozrah? this that is glorious in his apparel, travelling in the greatness of his strength? I that speak in righteousness, mighty to save.

Wherefore art thou red in thine apparel, and thy garments like him that treadeth in the winefat?

I have trodden the winepress alone; and of the people there was none with me: for I will tread them in mine anger, and trample them in my fury; and their blood shall be sprinkled upon my garments, and I will stain all my raiment."

(Isaiah 63:1–3)

Christ alone has overcome all spiritual principalities and wickedness.

The blood is not His own but theirs.

The Armies of Heaven: The Redeemed in White

"And the armies which were in heaven followed him upon white horses, clothed in fine linen, white, and clean." (Revelation 19:14)

These are not angels descending with weapons. These are the redeemed of Christ. They are clothed in righteousness, having been made clean by the blood of the Lamb. Their white garments symbolize holiness, and their following of the Rider shows that they share in His triumph.

They do not fight with carnal weapons. Their victory is their testimony. Their sword is the Word of God. As Revelation 19:15 declares, "And out of his mouth goeth a sharp sword, that with it he should smite the nations." This is not a physical sword, but the Word of truth that convicts, judges, and transforms.

The Rider on the White Horse: Christ the Conqueror

"And I saw heaven opened, and behold a white horse; and he that sat upon him was called Faithful and True, and in righteousness he doth judge and make war." (Revelation 19:11)

This is the risen Christ, not as the suffering Servant, but as the enthroned King. The white horse speaks of victory. He is not initiating conquest— He is manifesting it. His name, "Faithful and True," reflects His perfect obedience and covenant fulfillment. Revelation 3:14 calls Him "the Amen, the faithful and true witness, the beginning of the creation of God."

His eyes are as a flame of fire, penetrating all pretense (Revelation 1:1; Daniel 10:6). On His head are many crowns—not the anticipation of rule, but the evidence of it. This is the fulfillment of Matthew 28:18: "All power is given unto me in heaven and in earth." He received this power after His ascension after the resurrection (Revelation 4, 5). Jesus speaks as the risen Christ who returned to His disciples, not as a conqueror with a sword in His hand, but as the Conqueror with the Word in His mouth.

The Defeat of the Beast and False Prophet

This chapter is not about violence, but vindication. It is not about war, but worship. The King does not return to claim a throne—He rides from resurrection already seated upon it. The winepress has been trodden. The vesture has been stained. The judgment has been executed. The white horse has ridden.

This priestly unveiling mirrors Ezekiel's vision of the restored temple, whose glory would return not in stone and gold, but in Spirit and truth.

"So the Spirit took me up, and brought me into the inner court; and, behold, the glory of the Lord filled the house." (Ezekiel 43:5)

What Ezekiel saw in shadow, Revelation unveils in substance. The indwelling glory that filled the temple now dwells in Christ and His body— the Church.

Zechariah, too, foresaw the uniting of priest and king in one figure: "He shall be a priest upon his throne…." (Zechariah 6:1)

In Revelation, Jesus is both Priest and King—fulfilling what the prophets could only glimpse from afar.

Conclusion: Living in the Unveiled Victory

Revelation 19 is not a prophecy of a war yet to be waged—it is a vision of a victory already won. The Rider on the white horse is not galloping into battle; He has emerged from the tomb. He is not coming to claim authority—He is riding forth in the full glory of authority already granted to Him. Heaven opens not in anticipation of conflict, but in joyful declaration of Christ's coronation.

The white horse has already ridden. The blood has already been shed. The crowns have already been placed. We are not awaiting the reign of Christ—we are invited to live in it. This vision is our reality. Christ has triumphed, the Word of God goes forth, and the saints follow, clothed in righteousness, bearing witness to a kingdom that has come. He is King. He is risen. And He is reigning.

Key Takeaways:

Revelation 19 is a vision of Christ's completed triumph following His resurrection and ascension, and return to the disciples as the reigning King of kings and Lord of lords, not a future battle.

The "garment dipped in blood" and the "winepress" imagery reference Isaiah 63, symbolizing Christ's judgment upon the covenant-breaking system and people who rejected Him, rather than His own blood.

The "armies of heaven" following Him are the redeemed, clothed in righteousness, who overcome by the blood of the Lamb and the word of their testimony, sharing in His present victory.

Chapter 12

SPIRITUAL PRETERISM: A PERSPCTIVE ON REVELATION

The Transformative Lens: Spiritual Preterism Unveiled

As we near the end of our transformative journey through the Book of Revelation, we have embarked on a profound exploration of Spiritual Preterism.

This perspective allows us to delve into the depths of this sacred text, revealing mysteries often shrouded in symbolic language and apocalyptic imagery.

Our quest is guided by curiosity and a thirst for spiritual understanding, aiming not just to decode Revelation's symbols but to uncover the timeless truths hidden within.

Through this lens, Revelation becomes a living testament to the eternal presence of Jesus Christ in our lives.

Understanding Spiritual Preterism: Shedding Light on Revelation's Message

Our journey into Spiritual Preterism reveals profound connections, weaving together events, places, and symbols into a rich tapestry of spiritual insight.

This approach unveils the idea that Revelation is not merely a history lesson or a glimpse into the future; it is a timeless unveiling of Jesus Christ's role in God's divine plan. Like a mirror reflecting eternal truths, it shapes our understanding of the universe and our place within it.

Consider a modern-day believer facing personal trials. By interpreting Revelation through the lens of Spiritual Preterism, they can find solace in the text's message of hope and redemption. The symbols and prophecies serve as guides, leading them closer to divine wisdom and providing reassurance that their struggles are part of a larger redemptive plan.

Discovering Key Insights: Exploring Revelation's Riches

As we journey further, we encounter pivotal insights that shed light on the significance of Revelation's symbols and visions. These insights offer profound spiritual guidance and enrich our understanding of God's message.

We see how Revelation's core truths enrich our understanding. We witness Jesus as the earthly Messiah, the reigning heavenly King, and the path to the indwelling Spirit—inspiring us to remain steadfast in faith. We see the ultimate defeat of evil, a cosmic struggle culminating not in dread, but in the joyful inclusion of all people into God's family, a universal message of hope. This story celebrates Pentecost, the birth of the Church, as a new spiritual era, inviting us to participate in God's grand, unfolding plan.

Embracing Divine Harmony: Revelation's Symphony

Reflecting on the insights from Spiritual Preterism, we are struck by the harmony and depth of Revelation's message. It resembles a divine symphony, where each note and melody weaves together to form a beautiful tapestry of truth. Revelation is not just a book; it is a living testament to God's enduring love and presence in our lives.

Imagine an artist drawing inspiration from Revelation's imagery, creating works that convey the divine harmony and cosmic order described within its pages. This artistic expression becomes a form of worship, a testament to the timeless and universal nature of God's message.

As we heed Revelation's call to exploration, we're reminded that the time for spiritual awakening is now. We're invited to dive deeper into its mysteries, uncover new revelations, and grow in our understanding of God's timeless truths.

Cosmic Choreography: Revelation's Divine Dance

In Revelation's cosmic dance, we witness the majestic journey of Jesus Christ through time and eternity. From His earthly ministry to His heavenly reign, we are captivated by the beauty and wonder of God's divine plan unfolding before our eyes. This journey is mirrored in the lives of believers who find themselves part of this celestial choreography.

Consider a community choir performing a piece inspired by Revelation. Each member contributing their unique voice creates a harmonious whole that echoes the unity and diversity of God's kingdom. This performance becomes an act of worship, a reflection of the cosmic dance of grace and truth.

197

As Revelation's scroll unfurls, we're drawn into a celestial symphony of grace and truth, where each revelation resonates with the eternal truths of God's kingdom. It's a journey of discovery and transformation, leading us closer to the heart of God.

The Sealed Book in Old Testament Prophecy

In Isaiah 29:11 the prophet speaks of a sealed book: "And the vision of all is become unto you as the words of a book that is sealed, which men deliver to one that is learned, saying, Read this, I pray thee: and he saith, I cannot; for it is sealed." This passage depicts divine revelation inaccessible to human understanding, awaiting the appointed time of disclosure.

The imagery of the sealed book symbolizes the hidden mysteries of God's plan, the unsealing of the Revelation of Jesus Christ.

This prophetic anticipation finds fulfillment in Revelation 5, where the sealed scroll is ready to be unveiled by the worthy, resurrected Lamb, Jesus Christ.

The Angel Holding the Open Book: Another Triumph of Jesus

In Revelation 10, we encounter another symbolic manifestation of Jesus Christ through the imagery of an angel holding an open book. This angel, described in Revelation 10:1–2, holds a little open book in his hand, signifying the culmination of the revelation initiated in Revelation 5. Just as Jesus the Lamb opens the sealed scroll, the angel now holds the open book, representing the continued unfolding of divine revelation and the fulfillment of God's redemptive plan.

This imagery holds contemporary relevance, speaking to the ongoing revelation of divine truth in the lives of believers. Just as the sealed scroll of Revelation 5 was opened to reveal "The Revelation of Jesus Christ", the open book in the angel's hand symbolizes the accessibility of divine wisdom and guidance to those who seek it. In a world marked by uncertainty and upheaval, this imagery offers hope and assurance that God's purposes are being fulfilled and His ultimate victory is assured.

Conclusion: A Tapestry of Timeless Truths

This journey through Revelation has not been a theoretical exercise but a spiritual unveiling. In a world where fear often dominates religious expectation, we are called instead to live in the radiance of fulfilled hope. Spiritual Preterism is not just an interpretation — it is a living perspective, rooted in the finished work of Christ and the indwelling reality of His kingdom now present within us.

No longer do we await a distant deliverance, for the Deliverer has come. The veil has been torn, the temple filled with His Spirit, and the New Jerusalem has descended — not in stone, but in Spirit, abiding in the hearts of the redeemed.

This is the victory the book of Revelation reveals: Christ reigning in glory, His people reigning in Him. As we continue to grow in the grace and knowledge of the Lord, may this unveiled truth transform how we walk, worship, and witness.

Let us now live as citizens of the city not made with hands, whose light is the Lamb and whose gates never close — for truly, the triumph of Christ is not only written but now lived.

Key Takeaways:

Spiritual Preterism offers a transformative lens, revealing Revelation not as future prophecy, but as a living testament to Christ's eternal presence and fulfilled redemptive plan.

The book emphasizes that God's plan transcends time, leading us to discover timeless truths and encouraging spiritual awakening in the here and now.

Revelation culminates in the unveiled reality of the New Jerusalem—the present, indwelling Kingdom of God manifested through the Church—inviting believers to live boldly in Christ's accomplished victory today.

APPENDIX

A Gentle Comparison: Answering Questions

Answering Questions from a Futurist Perspective

If you have journeyed this far with me, I pray your heart has been stirred—not by a new theory, but by a renewed vision of Jesus Christ, triumphant and reigning now. I know that for many who love the Lord, the perspective in this book may be new and may challenge long-held beliefs, particularly those rooted in a futurist understanding of Revelation. That view, which sees Revelation as a roadmap of events still to come, was my own for many years. My heart was often filled with anxious speculation rather than reassuring faith.

This appendix is not meant to be a harsh critique or an exhaustive debate. This book's purpose was never to weigh every theory, but to lift the veil on Jesus. However, I feel it is important to gently address some of the most common questions that arise when comparing the spiritual, fulfilled perspective of this book with a futurist one. My hope is to provide a clear and peaceful bridge, showing how a Christ-centered, fulfilled view can answer these questions not with speculation, but with the finished work of the Lamb.

The Core Difference: A Future Roadmap vs. a Fulfilled Portrait

The primary difference between the two perspectives lies in when and how Revelation's prophecies are fulfilled.

Futurism generally reads Revelation as a detailed map of events that will unfold in the future, often centered around a final seven-year tribulation, the rise of a global dictator (the Antichrist), and a physical millennial kingdom on earth. It often treats prophecy as a cryptic countdown to be decoded by matching symbols to current events.

Spiritual Preterism, the lens of this book, understands Revelation as a symbolic and spiritual portrait of Christ's already fulfilled victory. It sees the dramatic judgments as covenantal reckonings against first-century apostate Jerusalem, culminating at the cross and ending the Old Covenant age. Its focus is not on a future catastrophe but on the present, spiritual reign of Christ and the reality of His Kingdom within us.

The Beast and the Antichrist

The Futurist View: The Beast is often seen as a future political leader—the Antichrist—who will rise to global power, deceive the world, and demand worship.

The Spiritual Preterist View: As this book has detailed, the Beast is not a future dictator but a spiritual symbol representing the system of legalism and works-based religion that stands in opposition to Christ's grace. The False Prophet is the apostate priesthood enforcing this system, and the "Image of the Beast" is the physical Jerusalem Temple, which became an object of false worship after Christ's atoning work was finished.

The Spiritual Benefit: This shifts our focus from anxiously scanning headlines for a future political villain to examining our own hearts. The "beast" of legalism can rise in any generation—in any church or heart that trusts in performance over the finished work of Christ. The battle is not "out there" in the future; it is a present call to live by grace.

The Mark of the Beast (666)

The Futurist View: The mark is commonly interpreted as a future literal, physical mark, such as a microchip or tattoo, required for commerce.

The Spiritual Preterist View: The mark is a spiritual symbol of allegiance. Just as God commanded Israel to bind His law as a sign on their hand and forehead (Deuteronomy 6:8), the "mark of the beast" signifies a heart, mind, and actions (forehead and hand) devoted to the legalistic system of the beast. It is the spiritual signature of those who reject the seal of God's Spirit, which comes by faith, and instead try to establish their own righteousness by works.

The Spiritual Benefit: This understanding liberates us from fearing technology or government mandates as the "mark." It calls us to a much deeper spiritual reality: ensuring our allegiance is to the Lamb alone, sealed by His Spirit, and resting in His grace, not our own striving.

The Great Tribulation

The Futurist View: This is understood as a future seven-year period of unprecedented global suffering, war, and plagues, from which the Church will be "raptured" either before, during, or after.

The Spiritual Preterist View: The phrase "great tribulation" appears in Revelation 7:14, where John sees a multitude no man can number from every nation, kindred, people, and tongue—clothed in white robes and standing before the throne of God. When asked who they are, the angel answers, "These are they which came out of great tribulation…" (Revelation 7:14).

This is not a depiction of judgment upon apostate Israel like the tribulation of Matthew 24. Rather, it points to Gentile believers, the nations grafted into the promises of God, who have endured suffering and are now shown in victory. The "great tribulation" in this context is not a single apocalyptic event, but a representation of the spiritual trials and redemptive struggle experienced by the nations as they turned to Christ.

This also echoes Old Testament prophetic imagery, where the nations were seen coming into God's presence after judgment and purification (e.g., Isaiah 60, Psalm 87, Zechariah 14). The white robes signify righteousness received through Christ, not national lineage.

The Spiritual Benefit: This interpretation removes fear around some coming global catastrophe and instead emphasizes a spiritual harvest—a victorious multitude that has passed through tribulation not as punishment, but as part of their redemptive journey. It shows that the Lamb leads both Jew and Gentile into victory, and that tribulation is not to be feared as destruction, but embraced as the refining journey toward Christlikeness and eternal communion with God.

What About the Rapture and the Second Coming?

The futurist "Rapture" theory (specifically a pre-tribulation removal of the Church) is a relatively recent interpretation. The classic scriptural passages, such as 1 Thessalonians 4:16–17, describe the Lord descending with a shout, the dead in Christ rising first, and the living being "caught up" to meet Him in the air.

This book's focus is that the symbolic judgments within Revelation were spiritually fulfilled in Christ. This does not negate the promise of Christ's ultimate return in glory to bring about the final consummation.

Conclusion: A Call to Rest in His Victory

"Revelation is not the Church's nightmare— This is her radiant song of awakening."

Ultimately, the lens through which we read Revelation shapes how we live our lives. For years, I lived under a shadow of dread, looking for signs of doom. But Scripture revealed that Revelation is not the Church's nightmare—it is her song of triumph. It is the song of the Lamb who has already won, a Kingdom that has already come, and a Bride who has already been made clean and white by the blood of the Lamb.

EPILOGUE

The Veil is Lifted

There was a time when Revelation felt distant, sealed behind symbols and fear—veiled by tradition, mystery, and misunderstanding. But over time, through Scripture and the Spirit's leading, something shifted. I began to see the Lamb—not as a future rescuer, but as a present Redeemer. The veil began to lift.

"Nevertheless when it shall turn to the Lord, the vail shall be taken away… But we all, with open face beholding as in a glass the glory of the Lord, are changed…"
(2 Corinthians 3:16–18)

This journey has revealed not dates and disasters, but a Savior. Not terror, but truth. The scroll is open. The Lamb is reigning. The Kingdom is here.

"And he opened their understanding, that they might understand the scriptures."
(Luke 24:45)

If this book has helped lift even a corner of the veil, to glimpse Christ more clearly, then it has served its purpose. We are not called to speculation, but to invitation—to see Jesus unveiled, the Bride adorned, the Kingdom alive in us now.

This unveiling isn't about having all the answers. It's about learning to see with spiritual eyes. It's about drawing closer to the One who holds the scroll, the Lamb who was slain, the King who reigns.

"And the Spirit and the bride say, Come. And let him that heareth say, Come… and whosoever will, let him take the water of life freely." (Revelation 22:17)

May this not be the end, but the beginning—of walking more fully in His victory, living as citizens of His kingdom. Praying to always see with spiritual eyes, and feel with an unveiled heart.

SCRIPTURE INDEX

Luke 4:18–19; 21:6

John 1:14; 12:23; 19:14

Acts 1:11; 2:1–4

Romans 2:12; 7:9–11; 7:24–25; 8:1–2; 8:37–39

1 Corinthians 15:19; 15:54–57

Galatians 3:10–13; 4:26

Ephesians 1:20–23

Hebrews 8:6; 8:13; 9:11–12; 9:28; 10:1–4; 10:12–14; 12:22–24

1 Thessalonians 4:16–17

Revelation 1:1; 1:5; 1:18; 2:10; 3:21; 5:1–10; 6:12; 7:14; 10:1–2; 11:3–12; 12:1–6; 12:10; 13:1–18; 14:4–5; 15:2–4; 17:1–18; 18:2; 18:10; 18:17; 19:1–16; 20:10; 21:1–27; 22:1–5

GLOSSARY OF TERMS

Apostate Jerusalem

The once-holy city of Jerusalem that turned away from God by rejecting Christ and embracing religious hypocrisy. In Revelation, it is portrayed symbolically as Mystery Babylon, the harlot who forsook her covenantal faithfulness.

Beast (of Revelation)

Not a literal monster or future world dictator, but a spiritual symbol representing legalistic religion, religious bondage, and the corrupt structures that oppose Christ's finished work. Often interpreted in this book as the embodiment of apostate Judaism and false religious authority.

Bride (of Christ)

The Church—the redeemed community of believers who are spiritually united with Christ. Revelation presents the Bride as the New Jerusalem, adorned in righteousness, living in the light of the Lamb.

Covenantal Transition

The divinely orchestrated shift from the Old Covenant (based on temple rituals and Mosaic law) to the New Covenant (based on Christ's atoning sacrifice and spiritual indwelling).

Daniel's Stone (Daniel 2)

The prophetic stone "cut without hands" that crushed the kingdoms of man and grew into a great mountain. Symbolic of Christ's spiritual Kingdom, which grows not by political force but by the Spirit.

Day of the Lord

A biblical phrase signifying God's intervention in human history for judgment or deliverance. In this book, it is interpreted as the coming of Christ's earthly spiritual judgment against apostate Jerusalem—not as a future global destruction, but as a covenantal reckoning.

Dragon

The great red dragon of Revelation represents Satan—the accuser, deceiver, and spiritual adversary of Christ's redemptive work. He operates through systems of legalism, fear, and counterfeit authority.

Futurism

A common interpretive framework that views the events of Revelation as entirely future—including a Great Tribulation, Antichrist, and physical millennial kingdom. This book rejects futurism in favor of fulfillment-based interpretation.

Harlot (Mystery Babylon)

A vivid image in Revelation 17 symbolizing apostate Jerusalem. Once the bride of God, she became spiritually unfaithful by rejecting her Messiah and clinging to a works-based system. Her judgment represents the definitive end of the Old Covenant age.

Kingdom of God

The spiritual reign of Christ, established through His death, resurrection, and ascension. It is a present reality for believers—"within you" (Luke 17:21)—not a future political regime.

Legalism

The reliance on the works of the law or religious performance to obtain righteousness. In Revelation, it is symbolized as the Beast's system—in contrast to salvation by grace through Christ's finished mission.

Lamb (of God)

Jesus Christ, revealed in Revelation as the Lamb who was slain and found worthy to open the sealed scroll. He is both sacrifice and King—the center of redemption and glory.

Mark of the Beast

Not a literal tattoo or microchip, but a spiritual symbol of allegiance to legalistic or idolatrous systems that oppose Christ. It contrasts with the seal of God, which marks those who belong to the Lamb.

Millennium

Traditionally interpreted as a future 1,000-year reign of Christ. In this book's framework, it symbolizes the spiritual reign of Christ from His ascension to the judgment of Jerusalem—a completed phase of redemptive history.

New Covenant

The covenant inaugurated by Christ through His blood, offering forgiveness, spiritual rebirth, and indwelling life. It replaces the Old Covenant and establishes a present, eternal Kingdom.

New Heaven and New Earth

Symbolic language representing the new spiritual order inaugurated by Christ. It is not a literal reconstruction of the universe, but the emergence of the New Covenant reality, where God dwells with His people.

New Jerusalem

The spiritual city of God—not a physical heavenly metropolis, but the Church, the Bride of Christ, made holy and radiant through union with Him. It is the city of eternal light and present inheritance.

Old Covenant

The Mosaic system of law, sacrifices, and temple worship given to Israel. It was temporary, pointing to Christ, and has now passed away with the coming of the New Covenant.

Partial Preterism

An interpretive position that believes most of Revelation was fulfilled in the first century, particularly the destruction of Jerusalem, but holds that some events—such as the final resurrection—are still future.

Preterism

From the Latin praeter, meaning "past." It interprets Revelation as describing events that were fulfilled in the past, especially in the first century. This book adopts a spiritually-focused form of preterism.

Revelation

The book of Revelation unveils Jesus Christ in His glory, not just future events. It reveals spiritual realities now present through Christ's redemptive work.

Scroll (Sealed Scroll)

The scroll in Revelation 5 symbolizes the redemptive plan of God. Only Jesus—the Lamb—is found worthy to open it. It is The Revelation of Jesus Christ itself. Its unsealing represents the fulfillment of prophecy and the transfer of covenantal authority.

Seal of God

A spiritual mark placed on the foreheads of God's faithful people, symbolizing protection, ownership, and covenant identity. Contrasts with the mark of the Beast.

Seven Churches

Seven actual churches in Asia Minor, addressed in Revelation 2–3. Symbolically, they represent the fullness of the Church under Christ's evaluation—highlighting faithfulness, compromise, and the need for spiritual renewal.

Seven Seals, Trumpets, Bowls

Symbolic representations of spiritual judgments, not literal global catastrophes. They unfold the process of covenant transition, revealing God's justice on apostate systems and His protection of the faithful.

Spiritual Preterism

The interpretive lens of this book. It holds that Revelation's events were fulfilled in the life of Christ, but emphasizes their spiritual significance—the triumph of Christ, the present Kingdom, and the indwelling reality of the New Jerusalem.

Temple (Heavenly)

The true dwelling of God is no longer a physical building but the presence of God in Christ and in His people. In Revelation, the Church becomes the Holy of Holies—the spiritual temple.

Tree of Life

Restored in Revelation 22, symbolizing eternal life and healing through Christ. It echoes Eden and Ezekiel's vision, now fully realized in the redeemed community of the New Jerusalem.

Two Witnesses

Symbolic of the Law and the Prophets, testifying to Christ's identity and mission. They represent the prophetic voice that calls Israel to repentance and validates the gospel.

Whore of Babylon

See Mystery Babylon. Symbolic of Jerusalem's unfaithfulness and rebellion against her covenant with God, contrasted with the purity of the Bride.

Zion

Another name for Jerusalem, often used symbolically in scripture to refer to God's holy dwelling or people. In the New Testament, Zion becomes a spiritual reality—fulfilled in the Church.

ABOUT THE AUTHOR

Tommy McNeill is a believer in Christ who, after years of wrestling with end-times teachings rooted in fear and speculation, discovered a clearer and more hopeful understanding of the Revelation of Jesus Christ. Having explored various prophetic frameworks—both popular and academic—he gradually came to see Revelation not as a forecast of doom, but as a victorious unveiling of Christ's fulfilled work and the ongoing reality of His spiritual kingdom.

This shift didn't come through tradition or external history. Tommy's writing reflects that journey—not as one who has mastered prophecy, but as someone led out of confusion by grace.

His hope is to serve fellow believers who are weary of fear-based theology and eager to rediscover the hope, clarity, and spiritual confidence found in Christ. He writes with the heart of a seeker, not a scholar.

www.ingramcontent.com/pod-product-compliance
Lightning Source LLC
Chambersburg PA
CBHW071726120626
46550CB00002B/402